FINANCIAL SELF-CONFIDENCE

A Woman's Guide

FOR THE SUDDENLY SINGLE

FINANCIAL SELF-CONFIDENCE

A Woman's Guide

FOR THE SUDDENLY SINGLE

Alan B. Ungar, C.F.P.

LOWELL HOUSE
Los Angeles

CONTEMPORARY BOOKS
Chicago

Library of Congress Cataloging in Publication Data

Ungar, Alan B.
    Financial self-confidence for the suddenly single : a woman's
guide / Alan B. Ungar.
      p. cm.
    Includes bibliographical references and index.
    ISBN 0–929923–38–3
     1. Widows—Finance, Personal.   2. Divorced women—Finance,
Personal.   3. Finance, Personal.   I. Title.
HG179.U45 1991
332.024 ' 042—dc20   90–28445
                                                      CIP

Requests for such permissions should be addressed to:

    LOWELL HOUSE
    1875 Century Park East, Suite 220
    Los Angeles, CA 90067

Publisher: Jack Artenstein
Vice-President/Editor-in-Chief: Janice Gallagher
Marketing Manager: Elizabeth Wood

Manufactured in the United States of America
10 9 8 7 6 5 4 3 2 1

DEDICATION

I dedicate this book to Cathy, my best friend and wife for the past 31 years, who was responsible for making this book intelligible. Not only do I appreciate her hard work on this project, I am relieved. Because she read the book so many times, she will know what to do when she is alone with her money.

ACKNOWLEDGMENTS

To my Wonderful mother-in-law, Catherine Chadwick, who after 20 years of library work and 70 years of incessant reading, was able to give me some expert advice.

To my peers who critiqued the book and kept assuring me of the need for it, and especially Ben Coombs, Jim Braziel, Kemp Fain, Ken Eliasberg, and Eileen Sharkey whose insights and suggestions were very useful.

To my friends at the Mid-Valley Racquetball Club who unwittingly provided incentive by constantly asking "How's the book going?"

To Brad Nave for his tenacity and good humor while helping with the final stages.

To my staff, Lida, Tina, and Janet, for being willing to put up with me while my attention was diverted "from business" and for helping to keep the office functional while the writing proceeded longer than expected.

To Ed Sherman (author of How To Do Your Own Divorce in California and Practical Solutions to Divorce) for his "nuts and bolts" ideas and appreciation of the book.

To Lenny Felder, Phd. (author and clinical psychologist) whose UCLA class "How to write a best selling non-fiction book" magically appeared when I most needed it and who continued to counsel me on an as needed basis.

To the group of people who volunteered to "beta" test the book by reading it to see if it was useful to them and reporting back what worked and didn't work. Thanks Carol Clark, Tasha Schaal, Jerry Caplan, Amani Fliers, Alvan Rosenthal, Janet Tribbe, Trudy Ahlstrom, Gaile Wakeman, Evelyn Ewing, and Karen Fink.

To my immediate family whose love, encouragement and interest kept me going.

CONTENTS

APPENDIXES

INTRODUCTION

This book is a tribute to my clients, whom I respect, admire and love. Their tenacity, openness and inner strength was, and continues to be, very appealing to me. I gain a great deal of satisfaction helping people who really want and need it.

All the case studies involve women. The subjects I am addressing, however, are not "women's issues". They are tools for anyone who wants to be fully responsible for his or her own finances.

One of the core themes of psychotherapy and other growth techniques is "taking responsibility" for your own life, your own actions, and your own happiness. This seems easier when we know that others have the same kinds of problems and when we can bring a certain amount of objectivity to our turmoil. After working through all the reasons for our unhappiness or discontent, we must still answer the questions: "What do we want?" and "What are we going to do about it?"

In order to know what to do about anything we must know our options. Without an understanding of the universe of choices, we are frozen in our fear of the unknown. The more we know, the more we are free to take action.

Because we depend on money for our survival, not knowing about it can be particularly debilitating. But there is only so much that you REALLY NEED to know in order to make money decisions with confidence. I have covered the important issues in the book.

When you are through you will not be a financial expert, but you will be able to make your own financial decisions. Don't worry if you find yourself getting bogged down or reaching "overload". Sometimes financial jargon can be a bit overwhelming, but you will get used to it. If you are stuck, take a break or just skip that part and come back to it later. It is not essential for you to understand every detail or to master one section before moving on to the next. If this is not a library copy, give yourself permission to underline, write in the margins, and dog ear the pages. I have tried to make the descriptions and explanations plain and simple, but some things persist in being complex. For this reason, you may find some of the exercises rather tedious at first. However, as you gain understanding you will find it less trying and may even begin to enjoy it. Some of my clients have actually been "turned on" by the process of gaining a real understanding of their finances. If, on the other hand, you find the details just too much, you will still be able to grasp the main points and should know enough to obtain and manage whatever assistance you need.

CHAPTER 1

ALONE WITH YOUR MONEY

Norma's husband, a Los Angeles police officer, was murdered while picking up his 5 year old son at school. Marilyn lost her husband after a prolonged acrimonious divorce. Although the conditions of losing their mates and how they experienced their losses were completely different, the processes of mending and the issues of money were the same.

While Norma had more money than she had before and Marilyn had less, each of them had to learn to relate to money differently from the way she had before. And although each of them had willing friends to help, they were each really alone with their money. Getting on top of their financial situations was critical to their mending processes, just as it is to yours. While neither of these women had all of the following concerns, each had some.

Can you identify with any of them?

"I DON'T UNDERSTAND MONEY."

"IT'S JUST TOO COMPLICATED!"

"I'M SCARED!"

"HE MADE ALL THE FINANCIAL DECISIONS."

"I HATE THINKING ABOUT MONEY!"

"IT'S TEDIOUS AND BORING."

"I'LL NEVER LEARN IT ALL!"

"I NEED HELP!"

"I WANT SOMEBODY ELSE TO DO IT."

This book is about alleviating those fears and getting on top of your resistance to dealing with money. Its focus is on helping you in very practical ways. It will help you understand that you are completely capable of handling your own finances. It will give you the tools to become comfortable with, and fully responsible for, your own money.

- You will know the eight things you should not do with your money while mourning.

- You will know the five things you should do with your money while mourning.

- If you have money to invest, you will know what rewards you can reasonably expect.

- You will know the four major reasons people lose money when investing and what to do about them.

- If you do not have enough money, you will have a good idea of what to do about it.

- You will know how to find what you own and what you owe.

- You will understand concepts such as "cash flow" and "net worth."

- You will know how to speak confidently to bankers and other possible lenders.

- You will know how to deal with annoying financial mail.

2

- You will be able to read those confusing mutual fund and brokerage statements.

- The financial part of your life will be organized.

- If divorce is imminent, you will have the tools to determine what you will need to make it on your own.

- You will learn techniques for figuring out what you really want your money to buy.

- You will be able to quantify your goals and figure out what you have to do to obtain them.

- You will have a basic understanding of those mind-boggling insurance policies.

- If you decide you do not want to handle your financial affairs by yourself, you will have enough information to help you select and manage your helpers.

- You will know most of the questions although you will not know all the answers.

Whether you were aware of it or not money was a key ingredient in your last relationship. It affected how you related to your partner, your family, your friends, and most importantly, yourself. Since money is tangible and quantifiable, it is perhaps the easiest part of your current turmoil to deal with. Other emotional aspects, such as your feelings of loneliness, loss, anger, and fear are more elusive and more difficult. So it makes sense to START the process of recreating your life by getting a handle on your money. I emphasize this point so strongly because it is easy to imagine someone (you?) saying, "I just can't cope with all that financial confusion while I'm feeling so depressed!" But if you wait until you have it together emotionally before you start to control your finances, you may very well compound your distress. Because when it comes to money, IF YOU IGNORE IT IT WILL GO AWAY.

Now that you are alone with your money, everything has changed. Not only do you have to change, you are now free to change! You have the chance to recreate your life in any manner you chose. The goal of this book is to facilitate your getting control of the financial part of your life so that you will emerge a stronger more self-confident person ready to take on the world.

CHAPTER 2

PROTECTING YOUR MONEY WHILE MOURNING

The loss of a relationship through death or divorce creates a period during which people must experience the various stages of mourning before they can get on with their lives. This process takes a different length of time and exacts a different emotional toll from each person, but the underlying dynamics are the same. When a relationship is lost, part of the structure which guides one's actions goes with it. Until this structure is rebuilt, the mourner and her money are very vulnerable. Often, long term decisions are made for the wrong reasons, decisions which can seriously impact the future.

Dr. Maurice Rapkin, an eminent and extraodinarily creative psychologist in southern California, suggests that when we lose a mate either through death or divorce, we experience a loss of aliveness, the sense of spontaneity and pleasure we associate with feeling really alive. There are many activities that contribute to this aliveness:

Breathing	Eating
Moving	Dancing
Exploring	Touching
Loving	Dreaming
Sleeping	Playing
Creating	Laughing
Socializing	Running
Singing	Joking

These spontaneous, pleasurable, innocent impulse actions are natural. Furthermore there are many ways in which we can try to facilitate these actions. Doctor Rapkin calls our desire to take these impulse actions "impulse wishes" and our desire to facilitate them "facilitative wishes." Often,we lose track of our impulse wishes, and the facilitative wishes become the end in themselves.

An example of this is the man who comes home from work to find dinner not on the table. Angry, he shouts, "Why isn't dinner ready?" His facilitative wish is that his wife have dinner ready. His impulse wish is that he is hungry and wants to eat. If he were in touch with his impulse wish he would see that he had options to satisfy his hunger. He could go to the refrigerator and get something to eat, or he could help get dinner ready. On the other hand he might not be hungry at all. He might just be tired after a hard day and want to go to sleep, but dinner always comes before bed; so he is angry without really knowing why. It is often very difficult to identify the actual impulse wish because it becomes so clouded over by varieties of facilitative wishes.

Money is a particularly confusing facilitator. It truly is useful in helping you get what you want and need when you are conscious of your impulse wishes and use money to facilitate them. But often people lose sight of the fact that the only thing money can do is facilitate; so it becomes an end in itself. The more money you have, the more you can buy. You can buy security, you can acquire things, you can go places, all because you have money. You begin to think that the more money you have, the happier you will be.

People who have money agree that it is easier to have it than not to have it, but they also agree that money and happiness are not synonymous. Spending money does not usually facilitate the satisfaction of such impulse wishes as loving, sexing, touching, sharing, and nurturing.

Relationships, on the other hand, do tend to facilitate those sorts of impulse wishes. So when you lose a relationship you enter a period of mourning characterized by a loss of aliveness. You die "little deaths." There is a sense of deprivation, sadness, and disorientation which makes you particularly vulnerable to the misuse of money.

If you are recently single as the result of a death, you might have more money than you had before, because of insurance. However, if you are recently divorced, you always have less. In either event your supply of money is limited and must be handled with care. The money you do have is an important cornerstone in the new foundation that you are building. It will be used to support the rest of your structure as you rebuild your life. Now more then ever you need support, you need nurturing, you need love, and you need relief from your deprivation and sadness. It is tempting to try to create security, to buy things that might make you feel better, to make fundamental decisions that you aren't ready to make, to use your money to alleviate your current emotional stress.

Spending money for going places or buying things can help. But unless you are in touch with your impulse wishes, and the money being spent is truly helping to facilitate those wishes, you will not feel satisfied. The danger is that you will spend so much of your money that the very cornerstone supporting your new foundation will disappear.

During your mourning period you will have to make money decisions. There is no way to avoid them. You can, however, avoid making major mistakes. You can protect your money while mourning by not doing any of the following things until you have had a chance to examine in detail the financial part of your life:

- Don't remodel your house

- Don't buy any life insurance.

- Don't invest because well-meaning friends have told you to.

- Don't invest in anything you cannot get out of very easily and at little cost.

- Don't spend money recklessly on nonessentials such as jewelry, new clothes, cars, or hobbies.

- Don't make costly decisions "for the good of the kids" if they are not good for you too.

- Don't give or lend money to relatives or anyone else even if you have a lot of cash.

- Don't borrow for longer than it will take you to read this book.

Any or all of these might be appropriate decisions to make eventually, but if they are made too early the results can be financially and emotionally disastrous. First it is important to understand your financial reality, your financial goals and needs, and your options. Here are some examples which illustrate this point:

MAKING DECISIONS FOR THE GOOD OF THE KIDS

For Betty and Bob the relationship was over before they actually worked out their agreement; so they were both in mourning as they divided up what little property they had. The major asset was the house. Betty insisted on the house "because the children needed the stability." However, the very decision that was designed to give them stability had the opposite effect. The alimony barely covered monthly payments and Betty very quickly fell behind. Distraught by the thought of losing her house, she became immobilized. Unable to find a job and miserable about the divorce, she grew desperate. Finally she realized that she had to sell the house. She thought she had considerable equity in it which could be used to get another place. But the market was soft and the house could not be sold for the value placed on it at the time of the property settlement. On the brink of foreclosure after nine months, she sold it for the existing mortgage plus her back payments. She lost her equity and finally rented an apartment for substantially less than what she had been paying before. Betty, who was a CPA by profession, was perfectly capable of understanding the ramifications of taking over the house payments when she settled with Bob. But because she was disoriented and in the middle of her mourning period, she wasn't thinking clearly. She made the decision "for the good of the kids."

When I questioned her further on the subject, she realized that it was she who needed the stability. She had not worked for two years and was nervous about going out on the job market. By doing it "for the good of the kids" she was unable to recognize her own impulse wish. If she had understood that it was she who needed the stability she felt her children needed, she might have realized the options she had to facilitate that wish. The house could have been sold while there was enough money to support the mortgage, thus avoiding the desperation sale. The equity taken out of the house could have been used to buy another less expensive house with a smaller mortgage. Or she could have let Bob have the house in exchange for other assets. By doing it "for the good of the kids" she did it to the detriment of both the kids and herself.

Of course your children need to be taken into account as you go through the mourning period. They are mourning too. They have impulse wishes also. But ignoring what you want and need by rationalizing that you are "doing it for the kids" can make you blind to your choices. The money part of your structure is important to their structure too. Often I have seen mourning parents spend money on their children instead of on themselves "because the children have suffered so much." This is natural and understandable, but the results can be severely unfortunate. The money is used up, the impulse wishes of neither the children nor the parent are satisfied, and a new foundation must still be built; but now there is less money with which to build it.

REMODELING YOUR HOUSE

Nancy and Norma had a lot in common. Both were LAPD widows. Both lost their husbands suddenly. Both were working wives and were comfortable with money. Both received insurance and pension money. Both were going to make it financially. One other thing was similar; when they came to me both were planning to remodel their houses extensively.

They liked the idea of creating a new environment, one which was of their own making. There was something appealing about not having to take somebody else into account when picking colors or making remodeling decisions. My experience has shown that often women in mourning want to move or somehow change their living environment. Impulse wishes to create and to be active are satisfied. Sometimes they feel better because they are doing something positive. A momentum can be developed which helps them in their healing process. As useful as this is, it needs to be approached with caution.

If either Nancy or Norma had spent the amount of money she originally had planned, the financial security of each would have been seriously jeopardized. They were lucky, the LAPD Family Support Group had counseled them to get help before the money was spent. After we worked out plans, which included looking at financial reality and future projections, each decided to spend less. Both did remodel, but they were still financially secure when the jobs were completed.

SALESPEOPLE DELIVERING CHECKS

Henrieta was 63 when Larry, her husband of 30 years, died. Their house was paid for, but they had not accumulated much during their lifetimes. She was very relieved when their insurance representative for the last 15 years delivered a check for $25,000. She also felt pretty good about buying another life insurance policy from him on her own life. She thought it would be nice to leave her children something.

The last thing Henrieta needed was life insurance on herself. By buying the policy, she used up some of the cash she had just received and committed herself to annual premiums. She was dependent on social security. She needed income! At that time, it was easy to earn 10% interest; so her $25,000 could have brought her an extra $200 a month, which she sorely needed.

Life insurance is for dependents, not for people who are dependent. People in mourning are particularly vulnerable to insurance salespeople who deliver checks. The check being delivered is proof positive of the value of life insurance. At this particular time in your life, you probably are not feeling very safe. The check helps and will make you financially more secure than you were, but buying life insurance will not make you safe. It will however, help your heirs. Though you may want to protect them, do it only after you have made sure of your own financial security.

ADVICE FROM WELL-INTENTIONED FRIENDS

John and Judy had a circle of friends whom they saw on a regular basis. Most of them were neighbors who bought their homes at the same time, had children of the same ages, and seemed to progress up the economic ladder at about the same pace. John died suddenly of a heart attack at age 44. Judy, 41, left with three teenagers, was without skills and had been out of the job market for 15 years. Fortunately there was a large insurance policy, as well as some accumulated assets and pension money. But Judy felt totally helpless with her money. Although she had paid the bills and balanced their check book, John had made the major money decisions. She thought she needed to make the money work for her, that it was unwise just to leave it in the bank earning passbook rates. However, she had no idea what to do.

Brad, a close friend, had recently made a lot of money in the stock market. Wanting to help Judy, he counseled her to invest the bulk of her money in some stocks that had done well for him. These were growth stocks that Brad was comfortable with and that had advanced substantially over the past year. Judy was grateful for Brad's advice because she knew he had made a good deal of money and because he was a friend whom she could trust.

When the market turned, Judy lost about 25% of her money. She was devastated, as was her friend, Brad. Judy's mistake was to think that because she could trust Brad and because he had made money in the market, his advice would be good for her.

Brad was a successful businessman who had dabbled in investing and had done well. He had a regular income and could afford to be an aggressive investor. He was not dependent on his investments for his security. Judy was. Since he was not a financial planning professional, he was drawing only from his own experience and his desire to help. He was not in a position to understand what she really needed.

The emotional impact of Judy's stock losses was even more severe than the loss of the money. She knew Brad meant well, but she was so upset about her loss that she could hardly talk to him. She became angry and eventually blew up at him as well as at some of her other friends. She was in the middle of her mourning period. Anger is one of the natural by-products of grieving, but her friends did not understand this. Eventually they drew away from her. She became isolated, alone with her mourning and her money.

Judy would have been much better advised if Brad had said, "Look, there is no hurry. Wait for awhile before you decide what you want to do with your money. As soon as you have had a chance to collect yourself, we will spend some time figuring out what you have and what you will need."

SPENDING WHILE MOURNING

Missing from Patty and Bob's relationship were impulse actions such as communicating, loving, and nurturing. They diverted attention from the central issues in their relationship by going on spending binges. Every penny was spent; no savings were created. The couple lived from hand to mouth in an attempt to fulfill their emotional needs. Although it provided a temporary respite, spending money could finally no longer shield them from the problems of their relationship. Patty attempted to involve Bob in therapy but he wasn't interested. They were divorced after thirteen years.

After her divorce Patty continued to spend money in an effort to feel better. However, she was running out of money. She had not changed her spending habits and there was substantially less to spend. She could no longer afford to try to satisfy her impulse wishes for loving and nurturing by buying things. When she came to see me, she was very much aware of her problem. She was proud of the fact that she had stopped spending extravagantly on herself, but the money was still disappearing. It turned out that although she had stopped buying for herself, she was continuing to spend unreasonable amounts on her children and on her house. She rationalized that her children shouldn't suffer and that the house was an investment. What Patty learned was that she loved the attention the sales people gave her when she went in to the store. She enjoyed creating, and she satisfied this impulse wish through buying things. When she recognized her impulse wishes, she discovered other ways to facilitate those wishes. Now she is enrolled in a fashion design class which will help satisfy her need to create. She spends less time and money shopping now.

It is not unusual for people to spend money to "feel better." This happens even when people are not in mourning, but the situation requires extra caution during the grieving process. Spending money on things you enjoy can supplement grieving but it is no substitute for truly mourning, for paying attention to how you feel and accepting those feelings.

13

GIVING MONEY TO RELATIVES

When John died, Sylvia received a $150,000 life insurance payment. The money was important to her since she and John had not accumulated much during their 35 years of marriage. They had, however, acquired 3 wonderful grandchildren whom she wanted to see whenever Barbara and Walter, her daughter and son-in-law, would allow it. Prior to John's death, Walter had started manufacturing women's apparel. Although the business was growing, cash was a problem. Two months after his mother-in-law received her insurance money, Walter asked her to lend him $50,000 to keep the business going. Sylvia loved her daughter, son-in-law and grandchildren. They were even more important to her now that John had died. So of course she lent them the money. Six months later Walter's business failed. Sylvia probably could have handled losing the money, but she lost more. Walter and Barbara, perhaps because of guilt, suddenly found her meddlesome and annoying. They began avoiding her and let her visit on special occasions only. She was essentially cut off from her grandchildren.

Sylvia's case is not unusual. It is very difficult to refuse help to loved ones who need money. However, unless you have an unlimited supply, it is best to wait until you understand YOUR financial situation before giving any of your money away. Tell those who are asking that you are not yet feeling secure about your financial situation and are not willing to lend or give any money to anybody until you do. If you have a very difficult time saying "No," use your financial planner, CPA, or attorney as the bad guy.

WHAT SHOULD YOU DO TO PROTECT YOUR MONEY WHILE IN MOURNING?

- DO WAIT. There is no reason to rush into major money decisions.

- DO KEEP YOUR MONEY SAFE. Keep it in a bank for a little

14

while in a 3 or 6 month C.D., money market, or even in pass book account. However, remember that banks and savings and loans only insure accounts to $100,000. So if you have more than that, use more than one institution. Yes, these instruments pay low interest, but they are accessible and they are safe in the short run.

- DO PROTECT YOURSELF. Make sure you have enough medical and disability insurance (see chapter 7 on insurance).

- DO BE AWARE OF YOUR IMPULSE WISHES. When spending money, ask yourself which impulse wish is being facilitated by your purchase. For the big purchases ask yourself whether there are other ways (besides buying something) to facilitate your wishes.

- DO REMEMBER THAT YOU ARE MOURNING. This does not mean that you are some kind of freak. It just means that you are particularly vulnerable right now and need to be especially cautious with your money.

You need time, education, and perspective before you make any major decisions about your money. It really won't take long and the next chapter will get you started.

CHAPTER 3

WHAT TO DO FIRST

The first thing to do is get yourself a container for files. A file drawer of some sort works best. You will need at least one drawer to begin with. Make sure that your container will hold Pendaflex type files. Buy at least 25 file folders, blank file folder labels and 12 to 14 Pendaflex files and tabs. Also get some "Post-Its" (those little stick-on notes).

Don't bother to read the rest of this chapter unless you are willing to start the organizing process. This chapter is about action and getting organized. Procrastination ends here. When you are finished, you will have accomplished the following:

- You will know what you own.

- You will know what you owe.

- You will have eliminated much clutter from the financial part of your life.

- You will know what to keep and what to throw away.

- You will know what to read and what not to read.

- You will know what to do with your mail.

- You will know how to read statements from stock brokers, banks and mutual funds.

- You will feel great about your progress.

16

SETTING UP YOUR FILES

Even if your prior mate was a very organized person, it is important that you have your own organization. You may feel perfectly comfortable with how he had things organized, but unless you were very involved with setting it up, it is still his organization. You need to have your own so that you will not have to think "Where would John have kept this?" as new information comes in or as you are looking for things. You are the one who is now going to make decisions and keep track of what you have; so make this organization YOURS!

The file organization I recommend below facilitates financial planning and uses that vocabulary. You may chose to have your own or expand on it. Whatever works is fine.

1. Start by setting up the Pendaflex files listed below. You may eventually want more, but these are the main categories:

ASSETS
ESTATE
INSURANCE
LIABILITIES-LONG TERM
LIABILITIES-SHORT TERM
MISCELLANEOUS
PAID FILES
SOCIAL SECURITY
TAXES

2. Decide into which major category each document falls. Later in this chapter there is more information about where to find the documents and how to categorize them.

3. Use the YES/NO technique discussed below.

4. Create file folders as necessary.

5. Keep a note pad handy. Filing is rather like putting pictures in an album. It is easy to get side-tracked. As you look at the paper work and questions pop up, or as things occur to you to do, write them down on your pad along with the name of the file. You can stick "post-its" on the documents for quick reference. You will then go back to get your answers all at once. Keep a separate TO DO file folder for your notes. This will enable you to continue with your central task, which is to get things organized.

Do not try to understand all the paper work that you are going through at this point. This first step is just for categorizing.

WHERE IS EVERYTHING ?

If you do not know what you have or what you should be looking for, here are some places to look.

1. In the case of a divorce, your "Marital Settlement Agreement" lists what is yours.

2. When there is a death, the probate and estate settlement papers will help.

3. Your tax return is very useful because all income must be reported to the IRS, and you can find here the names of investments you may have forgotten.

4. Checks and check books tell you who has been paid and what has been received.

5. Your accountant, tax preparer or business manager should be able to help you if you are unable to find records of your assets, liabilities and taxes.

6. Attorneys usually keep duplicates of estate document such as trusts or wills.

7. If a plan has been written for you by a financial planner, either find the plan or call the planner. Usually financial plans deal with all the major categories in your file drawer and contain a list of all the specifics in the plan.

WHAT SHOULD YOU THROW AWAY AND WHAT SHOULD YOU KEEP?

I had a client who once threatened to sue me if I did not do something about all the mail she was getting. Although she was not completely serious, she was serious. Every day she dreaded going to the mail box for fear of having to read through all her mail and make decisions. She felt as if she was being attacked by the mail. You might understand how she felt. Whatever the mode of communication, people are either trying to sell you something or give you information about what you already have. It is easy to handle the phone. All you do is hang up. But mail! For some reason it is more difficult to throw things away. There is something so final about it. After all, it could be something important. Or you may need it later! Most people save and stack every piece of paper they receive about their investments.

Because of this you probably already have more documents than you need. Additionally, with time and the mail, you will be getting more. Most people wait until they can't stand it any more and then just throw their stacks away. As the stacks grow one becomes increasingly annoyed at the clutter and anxious about having to face it sometime. Some people are so intimidated by these stacks, they consider moving to get away from them. Fire is another alternative.

But there is a better answer. Believe it or not it is easy. It will work for your mail and for all those papers you are filing. You will find that it is fast, simple and thorough. I call it the YES/NO technique.

You can think of it as a game. Here are the rules:

1. Do not pick up a piece of paper or open a letter unless you are willing to answer the listed YES/NO questions.

2. Do not put the piece of paper down until you have taken the appropriate action to your YES/NO answer.

YES/NO QUESTIONS

1. Is the purpose of this piece of paper to sell something? YES or NO?

2. If the answer is YES, the next question is "Do you want to consider buying it?" If the answer is NO, throw the paper away. If it is YES then put it in either a TO DO file or a THINGS TO CONSIDER BUYING file. The THINGS TO CONSIDER BUYING file is the devil that will eventually get you. No decision has been made and might not be for some time. That is O.K. Perhaps now is not a good time. However, eventually this file will get so big that you will have to go through it. When you do, use the same YES/NO technique to clean out the file.

3. Is this piece of paper asking you to take some sort of action, such as go to a meeting or vote on something? Is the requested action something you are willing to do? If the answer is NO, throw the paper away. If the answer is YES put it in one of the following files:

    a. THINGS TO DO IMMEDIATELY. Be sure to put it on your calendar also.

    b. THINGS TO DO LATER. This file has the potential for growing too. You will be putting things in it that you think you want to do, but aren't really sure about. That's O.K. When you pick the papers up again, you will be able to answer YES/NO.

4. Is this piece of paper giving you information that you will need at a later time? "But I don't know whether I will need it later, and I don't want to take any chances," you might say to yourself. By the time you are through with this chapter, you will know which pieces of paper you need to keep and which you need to chuck. So if you are in doubt, stack them until you finish the chapter.

If you are the kind of person who wants to create your own Encyclopedia of Interesting Information, buy a separate file drawer and keep it all in one place. Do not try to keep interesting information mixed in with your financial papers.

The YES/NO technique gets easier as you practice. Now that you are about to go through all the papers you and your former mate collected, you are going to get some practice. Before you do this, however, you need to understand what to look for and what each of the categories means.

ASSETS

According to our friend, Webster, an asset is "anything owned that has exchange value." The major assets that you might have are listed below. Each of these types of assets represents a sub-category which needs a file folder if you have that asset.

POSSIBLE ASSET SUB-CATEGORIES

BANK CHECKING ACCOUNTS
SAVINGS ACCOUNTS
CERTIFICATES OF DEPOSIT (CD)
MONEY MARKETS
CREDIT UNIONS
STOCKS
BONDS

MUTUAL FUNDS
PERSONAL RESIDENCE
REAL ESTATE--Other than Personal
LIMITED PARTNERSHIPS
IRA'S
ANNUITIES
PENSION PLANS--QUDRO's
PERSONAL BUSINESS
PERSONAL BELONGINGS
LOANS TO OTHER PEOPLE
GNMA'S
TREASURY BILLS OR BONDS

If you have more than two folders within a category, create a Pendaflex tab which says ASSET and then the name of the sub-category. For example, you might have a Pendaflex file labeled ASSETS--SAVINGS ACCOUNTS.

Many of your assets will be with banks or savings and loans. These financial institutions and the products they offer are very similar and are expanding. If current legislation passes, banks will be able to sell an even wider range of financial products such as stocks and bonds. For this reason, I have chosen to set up a filing system by type of account rather than by institution. You may prefer to do it by institution.

ASSETS--CHECKING ACCOUNTS

Write the name of the bank, "CHECKING ACCOUNT" and the current year on the file folder. If you have several checking accounts you should create a Pendaflex for ASSETS--CHECKING ACCOUNTS.

Banks will send you a statement at least once a month. This statement is very important because, in addition to your deposits, it lists the checks you have written by number, by date posted (when the bank posts them to its books) as well as the amount

You aren't the only one who makes mistakes; banks do too. By following the instructions on the back of the bank statement, you will be able to balance your check book and make sure that the statement is correct. You can tell how much you have in the bank, or at least how much the bank thinks you have, by reading the line that says "Statement Balance on _____(date)." If you have never had to balance your check book, put that in the front of your TO DO folder.

You should keep only one year at a time in your active files. If you keep more, your file becomes unwieldy. How long you save your statements depends on the laws of your state and Internal Revenue Service requirements. See appendix D for IRS guidelines. Three years is a good rule of thumb. However it is really a personal choice. I have not thrown any of my bank statements away for the past 10 years. I know it is stupid, but I admit to some paranoia when it comes to check records. I have this feeling that some day I may need to find how much I spent on something, or that I am going to want to prove that I paid for something. Ten years seems safe to me, but this one is up to you.

ASSETS--SAVINGS ACCOUNTS

Keep all your passbooks along with a master record of them in one file folder This master record consists of one piece of paper with the following columns:

Account Name	Account Number	Amount	Interest Rate	Maturity Date	Account Closed

For some reason, people do not like to throw away passbooks even when the account has been closed. When a savings account has been closed, banks stamp across the pass book "account closed." If you have books without this, you should check with the banks or savings and loans to see whether the account is still open.

ASSETS--C.D.'s

A C.D. is a Certificate of Deposit. It is a piece of paper or book which certifies that you have a certain amount of money on deposit with a particular bank or savings and loan. It states that the bank has borrowed money from you, is going to pay you interest for a specified period of time and will pay you back when that time is up.

I recommend that you keep a master list of all your C.D.'s in one folder, as you did with the savings accounts. The reason for this is that as your C.D.'s mature, you will need to make decisions about what to do with the money. Banks generally assume you will continue the C.D. for another similar period if you do not tell them what you want to do with the money within 5 days of maturity. It is quite possible that you may want to put the money somewhere else. Be sure to fill in the date the account is closed. After an account has been closed it is no longer necessary to keep that record. However, to play it safe you might save it for one year After that, it will just take up space.

If, while you are sorting out these papers, you run across a C.D. with more than $100,000 in it, put on your TO DO list that you need to change that. The reason is that bank C.D.'s are insured for only $100,000. An old C.D. which has been allowed to sit in one place for a long time could have more than $100,000 now, even though it didn't at the beginning.

WHAT BANK OR SAVINGS AND LOAN INFORMATION SHOULD YOU KEEP?

The mail from banks and savings and loans can be particularly dangerous. After all it is from THE BANK! Remember, although

24

banks are taking care of your money, their first concern is to make a profit; so they will try to sell you things. Use the YES/NO technique with bank mail also. You do need to keep your bank statements and checks (when they are sent, although most banks are trying to avoid sending checks). Deposit slips need only be kept until you receive a statement showing that the money has been posted. After that, you can throw them away.

ASSETS--MONEY MARKET ACCOUNTS

The advantage of money market accounts is that they pay interest, usually more than regular bank accounts with check writing privileges, and you do have check writing privileges. The number of checks you can write per month is usually limited, and the checks must be written for minimum amounts specified by the institution. Nevertheless, this vehicle can come in handy.

Banks and mutual fund companies offer money market accounts. Generally, banks have their money market accounts clearly labeled. This is not the case with mutual fund companies; the name of the fund may not say "money market" on it. A clue that a particular mutual fund is a money market is that the share price of a money market fund is usually one dollar and a dividend is paid monthly. Statements are sent monthly because dividends are paid monthly. So if you see a mutual fund statement which does not say "money market account" on it, but which does show a consistent share price of one dollar and monthly dividends, it is probably a money market account. if you are not sure, call the mutual fund company.

There should be some checks around for these accounts. If not, put in your TO DO File to contact your bank and ask for some. You probably will not need many, but you may as well have access in case you want it.

Keep all your money market funds together and title each folder MONEY MARKET followed by the name of the institution.

ASSETS--CREDIT UNIONS

In this file folder keep only your statements showing account activity. If you have borrowed from the credit union, you will be putting the loan information in the LIABILITY section of your file drawer.

ASSETS--STOCKS
and
ASSETS--BONDS

Here is an interesting mystery. You know that you own both stocks and bonds but you can't find them. Why not? Chances are that physical possession of these instruments has never been taken. When they were purchased through a broker, they were held in "street name." This means that the broker holds the stocks or bonds for you in the broker's name. This is done so that when you sell, the transfer of ownership is easy. If you do not have physical possession, then the way you know what you own is through a piece of paper called a "confirmation." Confirmations are sent by the broker when something is either bought or sold. If you have a confirmation which says that you or your mate purchased a security, but your broker's statement does not show it, it means that the security is not held in "street name" and that it is somewhere in your possession; or it has been sold, in which case there should be a confirmation for the sale.

If you actually have physical possession of stocks or bonds, you should not keep them in your file drawer unless it is fire proof and can be locked. A safe deposit box or safe would be better. These are negotiable instruments, which means that they can be cashed.

You can tell the difference between a stock and a bond by reading it. A bond will say this is a "debenture" or a "bond" and it will have a stated interest rate along with a specific date on which it will be paid back. Stocks will not have this information but instead will have words such as "equity" or "ownership" on them.

Whether your stocks and bonds are in your physical possession or not, create separate files for ASSETS--STOCKS and ASSETS--BONDS with the following information listed for each:

STOCKS

- Name of the company.

- Location of the stock certificates.

- Name, address and phone number of the broker or financial planner who sold it to you.

- Purchase date.

- Number of shares you own.

- Unit price paid.

- Total cost of original purchase.

BONDS

- Name of the company, municipality or government that issued the bond.

- CUSIP numbers. These are the serial numbers listed on the front of the bond.

- Location of the bond.

- Name, address and phone number of the broker or financial planner who sold this to you or to your mate.

- Date of purchase.

- The face value of the bond, that is, the amount the bond says it will pay back.

- The amount paid for each bond. This could be more or less than the face value depending on market conditions at the time it was purchased. To find the actual original price paid, find the broker's statement showing when it was purchased, or call the broker.

- Coupon rate (or interest rate--they mean the same thing). This is the interest percentage that is paid on the face amount of the bond.

- Payment period. That is, monthly, quarterly, semi-annually or annually.

- Maturity date.

- Sales charge.

All the information listed above can be found either on the confirmation statement or the first brokerage statement issued after the asset was purchased.

WHAT STOCK AND BOND INFORMATION SHOULD YOU KEEP?

When you own stock in a company, you receive literature and financial statements with information about the company. When you open the envelope, you need to decide YES/NO about whether you are going to read it. If you know you are not, then throw it away immediately. If you think you should, but know you won't, either ask someone else to read it for you or toss it. If you plan to at a later time, then put it in your TO DO file. After you have read it, keep the information only if you think you will need it later. Occasionally, you will be asked to sign proxy statements so that the company can elect its board of directors. If you have been paying attention to the company, you probably will have an opinion. If you do not have an opinion, call your broker and ask for some input. Be sure to send those proxies back. They are important to the management of the company you own and unless a sufficient number are returned, they have to keep trying. That is expensive to you as an owner.

HOW TO READ A STOCKBROKER'S STATEMENT

Usually, brokers' statements are divided into the following sections:

- Summary of Cash Balances. Summarizes the various types of cash accounts you have with the broker.

- Summary of Securities Held. Summarizes the value of the securities the broker is holding for you by category.

- Summary of Account. The summary of your cash balances plus the summary of securities held.

- Summary of Brokerage Account Transactions. Summarizes the transactions which occurred during the statement period indicated at the top of the statement.

- Securities Held in Account. Lists all of the securities the brokerage firm is holding for you, the number of shares, the share prices as of the date of the statement, total market value (price times number of shares), estimated income for the year, and estimated yield.

Most statements have full explanations of the headings on the back of the statement. If you do not understand these, call your broker. The account representative will be more than happy to help you. There is a chance that he/she will try to talk to you about your account and attempt to have you take some action such as buy or sell something. Just make it clear that at this particular time, all you are trying to do is to understand what you have and what the statement means.

WHAT INFORMATION FROM THE BROKER SHOULD YOU KEEP?

Maintain a file for each broker because every month you will receive a statement from each one. Statements from brokers show the current status of your portfolio and do not show history. For this reason keep any statement which shows when you have bought or sold something. You will need this information for taxes or just to keep track of how you are doing.

Always keep a copy of the CONFIRMATIONS (buy or sell advice slips) with your statements. If it is a recent confirmation, call your broker; you may need to send money or some may be due you. If you have the statement which lists the transactions for which you have confirmations, you can throw away the confirmations provided you have paid for your purchases. Brokers, too, will try to sell you things. Use your YES/NO technique.

ASSETS--MUTUAL FUNDS

Keep a file for each mutual fund, and if you have several different funds within a mutual fund family, create a Pendaflex for the family. You will receive statements only when there is some kind of transaction or at the end of the year. Mutual fund statements have a "Year-to-Date" format. This means that each time you get one, all previous transactions occurring in the present year appear on them. Most people have a tendency to keep every statement they get, and as a result, their files become unmanageable. So here are some guidelines for deciding which statements to keep and which to toss:

- Always keep the statement that shows your opening purchase.

- Keep the last statement every year

- Keep the latest statement you received for this year and throw the rest away.

HOW TO READ A MUTUAL FUND STATEMENT

Another great mystery of life is why mutual fund companies make their statements so difficult to read. It's as if they really don't want you to know what is going on.

The name of the mutual fund family is printed at the top. Next to that is another name which describes the particular fund within the fund family. For example, a statement from the Putnam family might say "Putnam Fund for Growth & Income," or "Putnam Government Fund." This is the name that you should use on your file folder, for example: ASSETS--PUTNAM--GOVERNMENT FUND.

If, somewhere near the top of the statement, it says "Monthly Withdrawal," this means that on a monthly basis money is being withdrawn from the account. To do this, the managers of the fund actually sell some of the shares and then distribute the proceeds to you. They will sell enough shares to meet your cash request. So if you have asked for $500 a month, every month they will send you $500 by selling enough shares to create that amount.

This system works well when the value of the shares is going up because fewer shares need to be sold to get your money and the value of your account may continue to rise or stay the same. However, it can be dangerous when the value of the shares is declining (you can tell this by finding the column marked "price per share" and comparing previous prices to the current one). Because more shares must be sold to give you the same amount of money, the value of your account will diminish. Stop your monthly withdrawals when the market has gone down for two months in a row, or when you think it is going to go down for a prolonged period. This can be done by calling the fund or your broker.

The remainder of the statement is in columns as follows:

- "Date"

- "Transaction" describes the type of transaction which took place on the date specified.

- "Account Opened" means this was the original opening transaction.

- "Cash Investment" means that more cash has been invested for additional shares.

- "Exchange In" means that more shares were purchased but the money used to purchase them came from another fund within this family of funds. Whenever there is an "Exchange In" there will be an "Exchange Out" in another one of the funds. An "Exchange In" is always done at net asset value, i.e. commissions are not paid. However, there usually is a transaction fee which will vary with the family of funds but typically is around $5.00. The fund will sell a share or a portion of a share to collect this money and this sale too will show up on your statement

- "Exchange Out" indicates that shares were sold and the money was used to buy shares of another fund within the family.

- "Shares Sold" means that some of your shares were actually sold back to the fund, and money was sent to you. This happens only when you instruct the company to sell. Most companies insist that a letter be written and your signature guaranteed (not notarized). Although this is somewhat bothersome because you have to go to a bank, broker or some other institution which can guarantee your signature, it is for your own protection.

Otherwise anybody who had access to your account number could write the fund using your name and instruct it to sell shares. The money could be sent to the writer at another address, thus defrauding you.

- "Dividend" means the fund paid a dividend and cash was sent to you.

- "Dividend Reinv" says that dividends were paid by the fund and reinvested in more shares of the same fund.

- The "Dollar Amount" column shows the total dollar value of the particular transaction.

- The "Share Price" column gives the value of each share purchased or sold on that day. This price will vary daily depending on the value of the stocks and/or bonds held in the fund portfolio on that day. The price shown in this column is either at NAV or at NAV plus a sales charge. NAV refers to net asset value, the market value of all the stocks or bonds held by the fund, divided by the number of fund shares. NAV is also called the "Bid" price. The NAV plus sales charge price is called the "Ask" price. If there is no sales charge, "Bid" and "Ask" are the same. So if your cash investment is $10,000 and on the day you make your investment the share price shown on your statement is $10 but you know because you saw in the paper that the NAV is $9.60, the difference is the sales charge. Most companies reinvest dividends and exchange in at NAV prices but not all do. To find this out, call your broker or the fund.

- "Shares This Transaction" indicates the number of shares that were involved in the transaction listed on the same line.

- "Share Balance" is the total number of shares you own.

I have no idea why mutual fund companies do not add a column which says "Dollar Balance." Perhaps they want to save paper or do not want to strain their computers. Maybe they just don't want you to know what your investment is worth.

To discover this, multiply the last "Share Balance" by the last "Share Price." So if the last number under share balance is 1946.659 (it usually has several digits after the decimal), and the last number in share price is 11.43, then the total dollar value in the account is $22,250.31.

WHAT MUTUAL FUND INFORMATION SHOULD YOU KEEP?

Mutual Fund companies will send you a lot of mail. They are constantly trying to sell you other funds. Use your YES/NO technique when looking through it. Keep the year end statements and toss all the interim statements unless the year end statement does not show all the transactions.

ASSETS--PERSONAL RESIDENCE

Keep in this file all relevant financial information about your house except your mortgage. Your mortgage is a liability and should be kept in the LIABILITY section of your file drawer. However, if the mortgage is paid, keep the records in your ASSET section. Keep your original escrow instructions in this file. It is a complete picture of the financial details of the purchase.

Be sure to keep all records of your home improvements in this file. These expenses can have a major impact on taxes when the house is sold. For example, if you buy a house for $150,000 and put another $50,000 in improvements, the cost basis of your house goes from $150,000 to $200,000. If you sell the house for $300,000 you will have to pay taxes on the $100,000 gain (the amount you pay taxes on is equivalent to the sales price less major improvements less your original cost). If you did not keep track of the cost of the improvements, you would have a cost basis of $150,000 and have to pay taxes on a $150,000. Keeping detailed records would have saved you about $15,000 in taxes (assuming 1988 tax rates).

ASSETS--OTHER REAL ESTATE

As with your personal residence keep all relevant information about the purchase and improvements of other real estate in this file. Keep leases in this section also. You can keep the daily management records either in this section or in a separate folder in the "MISCELLANEOUS" category.

ASSETS--LIMITED PARTNERSHIPS

Technically a limited partnership is not an asset. It is a method for buying an asset. For example, if you wanted to invest in some real estate, but did not have sufficient funds to do it on your own, you could pool your money with many other people in a limited partnership which owns real estate.

A limited partnership subscription agreement that is signed by you and/or your spouse is an indication that you own a limited partnership. File this document under the type of assets the partnership is investing in, such as real estate or oil. For each limited partnership you own, you should also have a prospectus. This is an important document because in it all known risks of the partnership are fully disclosed. Usually these are rather bland looking multi-paged documents on thin white paper with the word "Prospectus" on the front. Often they are stuffed inside fancy sales literature put out by the sponsoring general partner. If you cannot find a prospectus for a partnership you own, ask your broker or the general partner to send you a copy.

Every year you will be sent a K-1 from the general partner. This is a form you need for reporting your taxes. Instead of keeping your K-1's in this file, keep them in your tax file with the particular year reported. If you have access to a copy machine the K-1 could be kept in both files. Public limited partnerships are required to send annual financial statements. These should be kept. Although private partnerships are not required to send statements without a request, you have a right to request them whenever you wish.

ASSETS--IRA'S

IRA stands for Individual Retirement Account. An IRA is not an investment; it is a method for classifying investments. The classification was created by the U.S. Government as a way to give tax incentives to encourage saving for retirement. Although there are many IRA rules, the following are ones that could cost you money:

1. If you are younger than 59 & 1/2, there is a 10% penalty for early withdrawal, unless you have decided to annuitize, i.e., take regular monthly payments based on your actuarilly determined length of life.

2. All money put into IRA's prior to 1987 is subject to taxation when it is taken out, based on the tax bracket of the taxpayer at the time it is withdrawn. Because of the 1986 tax law, many IRA contributions will not be tax deductible in the year they are invested and therefore will not be subject to tax when the money is withdrawn. The rules about this are complex and should be discussed with your tax advisor.

3. All earnings built up in an IRA are subject to tax when withdrawn.

Keeping track of your IRA's may be confusing at first because it is possible to have so many different kinds. Mutual funds, stocks, bonds, limited partnerships, and C.D.'s can all be bought as IRA's. When these are purchased for an IRA account, they will have words such as "TTEE" (trustee) for "Jane Doe's Individual Retirement

Account" or "CUST FBO" (custody for the benefit of) written on them.

One way to keep this organized is to put all IRA accounts together into one sub-category. Another is to keep each IRA investment with its particular investment category. If you do the latter, clearly mark "IRA ACCOUNT" on the file tab. Additionally, you should keep an IRA file folder which contains a list of all your IRA accounts. There are a few occasions on which you need to pull them all together.

ASSETS--ANNUITIES

Because insurance companies sponsor annuities you might be tempted to keep these in the insurance part of your file drawer. However, an annuity is not an insurance policy; it is a contract that you enter into with an insurance company. The insurance company agrees to meet certain terms (that vary with different insurance companies and different kinds of annuities) and to pay you back the money you have invested. It is an investment that has many characteristics of an IRA. Here again, unless the account is annuitized (payments taken on a monthly basis for a predetermined time), there is a 10% penalty for withdrawal before age 59 & 1/2. Money accumulated in an annuity is tax-deferred and, as with an IRA, there are different kinds of investments that can be made within the framework of an annuity. If you have several different annuities, create a Pendaflex sub-category for them.

ASSETS--PENSION OR PROFIT SHARING PLANS
and
ASSETS--QUALIFIED DOMESTIC RELATIONS ORDERS (QUDROS)

All of these fall within the same category of assets because they have to do with pension retirement benefits. In a divorce settlement, a QUDRO is a method of isolating your share of pension profit sharing or IRA benefits. If, for example, there is $100,000 in your husband's pension plan and the divorce agreement is that you get 50%, a QUDRO separates your $50,000 from your husband's. If you choose to leave your half inside your husband's pension plan, then your share is protected by that order. On the other hand, you may wish to take your money out. You can do this without taxes by "rolling over" your share into an IRA account.

A Qualified Domestic Relations Order usually is part of the divorce document. I recommend that you photocopy this part of the settlement and set up a separate file for it.

If you have a pension plan of any kind you should make sure you have either a copy of the plan or a booklet describing it. You can get this by calling the personnel department. You have a legal right to this information.

If the plan was self-directed by your spouse, you can tell which are pension investments because somewhere in the registered name "TTEE" or the word "Trustee" will appear. All pension and profit sharing plans must have a trustee.

ASSETS--A PERSONAL BUSINESS

If you have anything in this category at all it will probably require a whole drawer or file cabinet of its own. However, in your personal financial file drawer keep a copy of all key documents, such as your stocks, partnership agreements, or corporate records. The originals should be kept in a safe place, such as a bank safety deposit box. Indicate on each file folder where the originals are.

A business financial statement gives an overview of the financial condition of a company at the time the statement is taken. If you have a personal business and do not know how to read a financial statement, and most people do not, include on your TO DO list a note to ask your accountant, attorney, or financial planner to help you. By understanding these documents, you will know what the assets, liabilities, and earnings of the company are.

Whether you are going to sell the business, operate it yourself or have someone else run it for you, it is imperative that you have a current financial statement.

Some people run businesses without having financial statements. If your former mate falls within this category, then you will have to determine the value of the business by reviewing past tax returns and the books. My recommendation is that you have your accountant create financial statements if there are none.

ASSETS--PERSONAL BELONGINGS

This is a catch-all section. Keep in here records of all major purchases such as automobiles, T.V.'s etc. If you borrow money to pay for any of these items keep only the record of your purchase in the ASSET section. You will be keeping your debt documents in the LIABILITY section.

This is the end of the ASSET category. Now put your ASSET files in alphabetical order.

ESTATE

In this section keep copies of your will and/or trusts. The attorney who drew up these documents has the originals. However, it is a good idea to keep copies in your safe deposit box also.

If you are going through the probate process, this is the place for extra copies of the death certificate and any correspondence related to the closing of the estate.

Now that you are alone with your money, your estate plan may need to change. Be sure to put a note to reevaluate your estate planning in your TO DO file.

INSURANCE

Maintain a separate file for each of your insurance policies. If you or your former mate has borrowed money from a life insurance policy, it is not necessary to keep that loan in your liability file. The money you have borrowed does not have to be repaid although you might choose to do so. It will be deducted from the face value of the insurance policy in the case of a death, or from the cash value buildup inside the policy if the policy is cancelled. Keep all relevant documents here with the insurance policy.

Often people do not throw away insurance policies which are no longer in force. This is not a good practice because, not only will old policies take up space in your file, you might think you have more insurance than you actually have. The best approach is to set up a file for each policy and then write the companies to see which policies are still in force. When you write, include the policy number because the company needs this as a reference. If you know the agent, just call and ask.

If he wants to present you with more or different insurance, let him know that you are not ready to make insurance decisions yet; all you are trying to do is determine what you have and what you do not have.

Now alphabetize your insurance files.

LIABILITIES--LONG TERM

If you do not know what debts you have and you have found no paper work to indicate that you have any, look in the check book for payments that are made on a regular basis. Additionally, there is a section in Schedule A of your tax return entitled "Interest You Paid" which will list the names of people who received interest from you in the last year. These names will help you find out to whom you owe money.

With any luck at all the LIABILITY section of your file drawer will be small. A liability in the accounting sense is any debt for which you are responsible. Nothing else needs to be in these files except information which is relevant to paying off your debts.

For example, in your HOME MORTGAGE file, you need to keep copies of the documents which define your mortgage. Mortgages can cause some confusion because usually no specific document proclaims itself as a "mortgage." A mortgage is an all encompassing term describing the major liability you have on your house. This liability has a NOTE and a DEED OF TRUST. The note is a promise to pay a lender such as a bank or mortgage company a certain amount of money over a defined period of time with defined interest charges and monthly payments. This note is secured by something called a "DEED OF TRUST." A DEED OF TRUST gives the lender the right to take back the property if you do not meet the terms of the note (the property is collateral--a kind of backup for the note).

Keep both the original NOTE and DEED OF TRUST in a very safe place (such as a safe deposit box) while the copies go in your HOME MORTGAGE file. If you are paying your mortgage with checks, and are saving the checks, it is not necessary to keep a separate record of your mortgage payments. At the end of each year, you will receive from the mortgage company a statement which tells you what portion of your payments were for interest and how much was applied to reduction of the loan. You should keep a copy of this annual statement in your home mortgage file as well as in the appropriate tax file.

For future planning, you will also need the following information:

1. The origination date of the loan.
2. The date the loan will be paid off.
3. The interest rate.
4. Whether the interest rate is fixed or variable.
5. If it is variable, the maximum amount that can be charged.

6. Whether there is a balloon payment at the end, and if so, how much.
7. The monthly payment amount.
8. The amortization schedule. This shows the schedule of interest and principal being paid.
9. Whether the loan is assumable.

The answers to these questions all appear on your loan documents, but they also can be answered by the company which holds the mortgage. When you call, have your loan number ready because that is the first question they will ask.

If you owe money on an automobile and the payee does not provide you with tear off stubs, in your AUTO LOAN file keep a running record of your payments. The column headings would look like this:

Date	Check #	Amount Paid	Balance Due

By maintaining a running balance, you will be able to track the progress you are making in paying off your loan.

Keep similar records for all major debts. Now alphabetize these files.

LIABILITIES--SHORT TERM (BILLS)

An ACCOUNTS PAYABLE file folder is a good place to put all of your bills as they arrive in the mail (though you may prefer to pay them as they come in). This file should contain no advertisements, only the bills and the self-addressed envelopes for mailing the payments.

MISCELLANEOUS

This is where you keep your special files such as TO DO, BUDGET, PAYCHECK STUBS, and THINGS I WANT TO BUY. Sometimes you may be holding a piece of paper that doesn't belong in any of the other sections that you have created. Good old MISCELLANEOUS will save you. Be careful of this section though. Most of it will represent procrastination or indecision. So as long as you are keeping the rest of your financial records in order and uncluttered, a little mess won't hurt. This section is like a garage, a great catch all, and makes you feel so good when it is cleaned out.

Alphabetize your MISCELLANEOUS files.

PAID FILES

This category contains your paid bills, filed alphabetically by payee. As you pay bills, mark your check number and date on the statements you retain for your records, and keep them here. At the end of a year, move all these into a storage container or throw them out if you can do that. If you do not pay by check, save the records for at least three years.

SOCIAL SECURITY

If you receive social security benefits keep your social security records in this file. If you receive Medicare or disability insurance money keep these records in separate files within this category.

TAXES

Keep your tax records in separate file folders by year. All receipts and records used to determine your taxes need to be kept for at least three years with the tax returns. After that you can throw them away but you should retain your returns. You should also have a file called CURRENT YEAR TAX INFORMATION. This file is used for business expenses, receipts and other records relating to charitable contributions, and any other items you will need for your tax returns.

Institutions with whom you have invested will start sending you 1099's toward the end of the year and K-1 forms will start arriving at the start of the next year. These same forms have been sent to the government by the people who have paid you interest during the year or have paid you for work for which they did not withhold taxes. Keep these forms in your CURRENT YEAR TAX INFORMATION.

As you will discover later, the data needed for filing your taxes can also be very useful in other ways, particularly in discovering your sources of income and your investments.

Each year the government sends booklets describing how to calculate your taxes. These are helpful if you are doing your own taxes but are space hogs after you are done. Because they are so official looking people have a tendency to hang on to them, but after the year of filing your return they are unnecessary and should be tossed.

Well, congratulations! You have taken the first step in being "alone with your money." Although you may not understand everything yet, you are in a better position to describe your current financial reality. And this is what we will do next.

CHAPTER 4

YOUR FINANCIAL REALITY

If the notion of discovering your true current financial status strikes terror in your heart, you are not alone. Otherwise rational people often avoid examining their finances because they think that if they know the real state of affairs, they will have to deprive themselves of things they want or work three jobs to obtain more income. So they put it off until the situation is so bad there is no choice. Unfortunately, by that time what may previously have been a relatively easy question of positioning becomes a severe and painful shock, and a radical change of life style.

Ironically, it is the very process of looking at financial reality which can alleviate fear. In my experience, even when the news is bad, people feel relieved after they have faced up to it. In any case, until you first look at your current reality, you will find it difficult to improve your circumstances.

Joy's case is a good example. For years Joy remained married to Don because she did not see how she could make it financially on her own. Although they both worked, their combined incomes were barely enough to cover expenses. When Joy finally looked at her financial situation she discovered that, even though her income as a single would be one third of what their combined incomes had been, if she made certain changes in her life style, she could survive. Without further hesitation, she initiated a divorce. She now shares a condo with two other people instead of a house with her husband, and for a lot less money. She now drives a car which is not as fancy as the one she drove with Don, but it is paid for. She still lives from paycheck to paycheck but she now budgets her money and doesn't live beyond her means. She has given up some of the material comforts she had before, but she is much happier.

Even if she had looked at her financial reality sooner, she might not have been ready for a divorce, but at least she would have seen her options. Before, what she had was a fantasy that she couldn't make it on her own. By looking at the numbers she was able to switch from a negative vision to a positive one. This gave her the incentive to take action.

Lidia's case is an example of how easy it is to become stuck in old behavior patterns not justified by current reality. Four years after her husband's death she still had a "poor me" attitude which she had acquired during their marriage.

While her husband was alive Lidia worked with him in their small printing business. Although she earned some of the money, she made none of the money decisions. Larry dominated in the financial as well as most other areas of their lives. Her "poor me" attitude gained her attention and sympathy. None of her friends could understand why she stayed married.

After Larry's death, Lidia did have a mourning period, but it was short. She was finally free to do what she wanted, when she wanted, without getting Larry's permission. No longer was she judged or intimidated by him. As happy as she was, she still had a "poor me" attitude. She thought she was poor because her income was less than it was when Larry was alive. She was still getting attention and sympathy because people believed that she was truly poor.

When she started spending her capital she finally became frightened enough to get help. At first she wanted me to assume Larry's old role, that is, to tell her what to do, make her investment decisions and give her permission with her money. After we took a good look at the reality of her financial situation we discovered that there was more than enough capital to be positioned to create income. With some encouragement, she not only realized that she could make her own decisions, she wanted to. She shed her "poor me" attitude and took control of her life.

If Lidia had been willing to look at her financial reality earlier, she would not have spent so much time feeling poor. Both she and Joy were able to make significant real life changes because they faced their money realities.

Understanding your financial reality can be the catalyst for non-financial changes in you life too. Once you understand what you own and what you owe, and what your expenses and income are, you will gain control of an important portion of your life. You will be able to make changes with confidence. Taking control of one part of your life will help you get on top of the rest of it.

In Chapter 3 you learned what data needed to be collected. Now you are going to learn what it means. By treating the following pages as a workbook, actually collecting the data and doing the calculations, you will eliminate much of your financial vulnerability.

YOUR NET WORTH

Net worth is a measure of your financial strength. It is calculated by adding up all your assets and subtracting all your liabilities. You want this number to be positive, and the bigger it is the better.

However, just because your net worth is big does not necessarily mean you have a lot of money. For example, if all you own is your house with a market value of $200,000 and a mortgage of $50,000 you have a net worth of $150,000. This net worth, however, is illiquid (cannot be spent) unless the house is sold, or unless you are able to borrow using the equity in your house as collateral.

By evaluating your situation in terms of your net worth you will be using the same language as others who are in a position to advise you or lend money to you. A sample NET WORTH STATEMENT follows and a blank form for your use is in Appendix E. You will notice that many of the items are the same as your file folder labels.

SAMPLE NET WORTH STATEMENT

DATE_____

ASSETS	SAMPLE AMOUNT	YOUR AMOUNT
Checking Account	$500	_____
Savings Accounts	5,000	_____
Money Market	10,000	_____
Certificate of Deposits	15,000	_____
Annuities	0	_____
Cash Value in Life Insurance	0	_____
Stocks	0	_____
Bonds	0	_____
Mutual Funds	20,000	_____
Municipal Bond Trusts	0	_____
Treasury Bills or Bonds	0	_____
Personal Residence	200,000	_____
Real Estate Other than Personal	0	_____
IRA's	16,000	_____
Vested Pension Plans	100,000	_____
Deferred Compensation	0	_____
Personal Business	0	_____
Personal Belongings	15,000	_____
Personal Loans	0	_____
Other Assets	0	_____
TOTAL ASSETS	**$381,500**	_____

LIABILITIES		
Residence Mortgage	$50,000	_____
Other Mortgages	0	_____
Credit Cards	1,000	_____
Bank Loans	0	_____
Margin Accounts	0	_____
Other Loans	0	_____
Other Debts	0	_____
TOTAL LIABILITIES	**$51,000**	_____

NET WORTH (Assets minus Liabilities)	$330,500	_____

HOW TO CREATE YOUR NET WORTH STATEMENT

The most difficult part is gathering the information. However, if you have set up your files as outlined in Chapter 3, you will find this relatively easy. The next section tells you where to find the various entries and how to use them. If you become stuck anywhere, just write a note to yourself with the page number showing where you got lost, and put it in your TO DO file. Research it after you have had a chance to go through the whole exercise.

YOUR TAX RETURN

A good place to start, when you are not sure of what you have, is with our old friend the tax return. If you cannot find your tax returns, go to your local IRS office and ask for form 4506. This filled out form along with $4.25 will get you a copy of past tax returns. Remember, you are dealing with a government agency; so allow plenty of time to get your copies. Also, if you are not yet single and for some reason do not want your spouse to know that you are getting copies of the return be sure to have the IRS send them to a different address.

Because all income and losses must be reported to the IRS, the assets and liabilities which generate income and loss will show up on your tax returns.

For example, if you cannot locate your savings accounts, CD's, bonds, or other interest bearing accounts, you can track them down via Schedule B of your tax return. Schedule B summarizes all the taxed interest and dividend income you receive. The letter designations could change in future years, but all the information will be on the return somewhere. Part 1 of Schedule B lists the names of all parties from whom interest is received. This schedule will show you how much interest has been paid to you, but it will not tell you the size of the asset which created the interest. For that you must locate the latest statements from the companies listed, or call the companies themselves.

Part 2 of Schedule B lists the companies that are paying dividends. This part of your tax return will show the names of mutual funds, individual stocks and money market funds. Again you must find the statements for these companies to discover the value of each asset.

Interest on municipal bonds will not show up on federal tax returns because the federal government does not tax them. Check your state return to see if any interest on municipal bonds is being taxed since states will tax this interest when they are not from the state in which you live.

Schedule C will tell you about any personal business you may own which is not a corporation. Unfortunately, it will not tell you what the value of the business is. You need current financial statements, as discussed in Chapter 3.

Schedule D shows assets which were sold for a profit or loss. So if you thought you owned something and cannot find a record for it, it may have been sold and should show up on this schedule.

Schedule E will provide the clues about limited partnerships or real estate that you own (other than your residence). Part 1 of Schedule E is for reporting rental and royalty income or loss. The names of all the properties producing income or losses appear on the first part of the form. Once you have these names you need to track down the paper work which will show you from whom the properties were bought, where they are, and who is managing them. You can then make calls to obtain the current value of your properties. Part 2 of schedule E will give you information on income or losses created from partnerships, S corporations, estates, or trusts. The names on the schedules will assist you in locating the people who can help put a value on these investments.

K-1 forms (usually found with your tax returns, although not attached) report more detailed information on estates, trusts, or partnerships. You probably will need your accountant or financial planner to help you understand these. K-1's are quite difficult to interpret even for sophisticated investors.

One common investment shown on a K-1 is the limited partnership. To get some idea of the value of this investment talk to the general partners. If you do not know who they are, ask the person who sold it to you. Partnerships should be listed on your NET WORTH STATEMENT under the type of investment. For example, a real estate limited partnership would go under "Real Estate--Other Than Personal."

STATEMENTS FROM MUTUAL FUND COMPANIES

Instructions for calculating the value of your mutual funds were given in Chapter 3. Because stock prices vary and your statements may be old, it would be a good idea to call the mutual fund company to get your current share balance and share price (NAV). Almost all mutual fund companies have "800" phone numbers. When you call, the person trying to help will ask for your account number, but if you do not have that your social security number will do. Remember that there is no reason to be intimidated; the people on the other end are trained to help people understand their statements, and most people need help! Add the current value of all your mutual funds and enter the total in the mutual fund section of your NET WORTH STATEMENT.

STATEMENTS FROM YOUR BROKERS

There is more useful information on a broker's statement than there is on a mutual fund statement. However, for the same reason, these statements can be formidable to read. Chapter 3 contains details on how to do this. You might prefer instead to call and ask for help from the salesperson who sold you the securities. The danger in doing this is that you will probably be told about new investments and given suggestions on what to do with what you have. Perhaps at a later time you will want this information, but for now, all you want to do is get what you need to fill out your NET WORTH STATEMENT.

YOUR RESIDENCE

For purposes of your NET WORTH STATEMENT, the value of your real estate is equal to its current market value. To obtain this figure, check around your neighborhood to see whether any houses are for sale. If so, call the real estate office representing the seller. Tell them you live in the same neighborhood and would like to get a comparable price for your house. Because they have just done "comps" for your neighbor and because they are always looking for more customers, they will be happy to give you the information. Don't be tempted to sell your house now, however.

REAL ESTATE OTHER THAN PERSONAL

If you own other real estate, obtain comparable prices the same way. Another "quick and dirty" way to estimate the value of your rental properties is through the use of a capitalization rate. See appendix A for an explanation of this concept.

IRA'S

Add the value of all the IRA's in that section of your file drawer and enter the total on the NET WORTH STATEMENT.

VESTED PENSION PLAN AND QUALIFIED DOMESTIC RELATIONS ORDERS

To be vested means to have a right to assets which cannot be taken away from you. People become vested in pension plans after they have worked for a company for a specified period of time. To find the value of the vested portion of your pension plan call the personnel department of the company offering the plan.

If the pension plan was self-directed by your former mate and you have no idea of the assets inside the pension plan, find out who the plan administrator is. Plan administrators do all the relevant paper work for a corporation's pension plan, including reporting on assets. The corporation accountant can tell you who the plan administrator is. The plan administrator will also be able to tell you through whom the investments were purchased so that you can call those people to get more information should you need it.

If you have a QUDRO, as discussed in the previous chapter, you can get information about it also from the plan administrator.

DEFERRED COMPENSATION

Sometimes corporations defer income for employees through plans such as 401'k's, thrift plans, ESOP's, and stock options. The employee, instead of taking all of his or her pay, defers payment to a later time. Often companies will contribute matching funds to these deferrals. Many times in case of death these funds are paid automatically, but not always. If you are alone because of death, you need to be sure you have contacted your spouse's company to find out about deferred compensation and include these asset amounts on your NET WORTH STATEMENT.

PERSONAL BELONGINGS

Determining the value of your personal chattels requires rough estimates of the worth of furniture, jewelry, records, T.V.'s, etc. When trying to estimate this figure, think in terms of what you could get for these items if you sold them.

LIFE INSURANCE CASH VALUE

Some life insurance policies have a "cash value," which means that the cash which has accumulated belongs to the owner of the policy. This is cash that you could get either through cancelling the policy or by borrowing. It is therefore an asset. The policy might also have "dividends" which should be considered an asset. Though dividends cannot be borrowed you can cash them out (without cancelling the policy). If you see something called "paid up additions" this too is an asset. It represents cash value that can be used to buy more insurance, it may be borrowed against, or it will be received if the policy is cancelled.

Most insurance polices are impossible for the lay person to understand. Your insurance salesperson will get you that information. However, when you ask, make it clear that you are only getting the information for purposes of your financial statement. You may want to obtain more insurance later, but now all you want is information.

PERSONAL BUSINESS

A business is worth what somebody is willing to pay for it. So unless and until you sell it, you can only estimate its value. To do this you will need professional help. Your accountant or financial planner can assist with this. Do not assume that the business is worth nothing because your spouse is no longer there to run it. It may be worth less, but there still could be assets such as inventory, equipment, furniture and customers which are saleable. For example, if a one man office CPA were to die, his clients would still need to be serviced. Somebody might be willing to pay for these clients.

LIABILITIES

RESIDENCE AND OTHER MORTGAGES

For most people, a home mortgage is the largest liability. Often the principal remaining to be paid is noted on the payment slip, but if not, call the mortgage company and get the amount. This is the figure that goes in the NET WORTH STATEMENT under LIABILITIES. The remaining principal on any other real estate mortgage should be listed as an "Other Mortgage." One mortgage to be particularly aware of is a home equity loan. These are loans which have been taken out using the equity in your home as collateral. Often they are open ended loans, which means they are not being paid off (or amortized) on a regular basis. As long as the interest is paid, the lending institution (usually a bank) is not concerned about the principal. However, if you sell your house, the loan would have to be paid off. Since this lability is separate from the underlying note in your original mortgage, it should be kept in a separate file.

CREDIT CARDS

Just enter the total that you owe on all credit cards.

BANK LOANS

Call the bank, ask for the loan department, give your loan number and they will tell you the balance due. Enter this total on the NET WORTH STATEMENT.

MARGIN ACCOUNTS

A margin account is an account that is used when stocks or bonds are bought with credit. This happens when an investor does not want to pay cash for the stocks purchased. The brokerage firm will usually lend up to 50% of the value of a portfolio. So, if a client owns $100,000 worth of stock free and clear, the brokerage firm will lend the client $50,000 to buy additional stock. Interest is paid on this debt, and the loan itself must be paid back eventually. Any amount you owe on margin will appear on the broker's statement and should be entered in your net worth statement under LIABILITIES.

You have to be very careful with these accounts, because if the market changes and the equity in the account is less that 50% of the value of the portfolio, the broker will make a "margin call." This means that they will ask for enough cash to bring the value of the portfolio up to required limits. If the margin call is not met within a specified time, the broker will sell off some of the remaining assets in the portfolio to satisfy the legal requirements. Sometimes this can happen with disheartening rapidity as in the crash of October 1987. The market moved so quickly that brokers did not have time to contact their clients and clients were notified after their assets had been sold! Margin accounts are for sophisticated investors who are actively managing their account. If you do not fit that profile, you should figure out (with the help of your financial planner or broker) the most efficient way of paying off the account.

OTHER LOANS AND OTHER DEBTS

These are located in your LIABILITIES--LONG TERM files. All you need for the NET WORTH STATEMENT is the total amount still owing.

HOW TO CALCULATE YOUR NET WORTH

Subtract TOTAL LIABILITIES from TOTAL ASSETS, as shown on the sample NET WORTH STATEMENT. This is a measure of your financial health as of the date the information was collected. Be sure to put that date on your statement. Your net worth will grow or diminish in the future, depending on what you do from now on. This net worth part of your financial reality is affected by your cash flow, which is the next thing we will address.

YOUR CASH FLOW

"Cash Flow" is the financial term for the difference between income and expenses. It is intimately related to your net worth. When your cash flow is positive, your net worth will increase. When it is negative, your net worth will decrease.

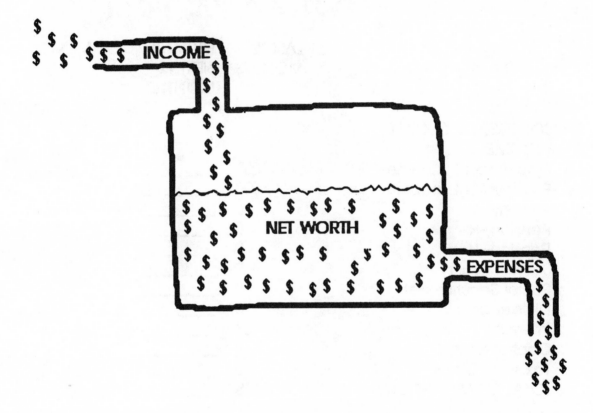

You probably know already whether your cash flow is positive or negative. That is, you know whether you are spending more than you have coming in. Now you need to get control of the details of the flow. To do this fill out the CASH FLOW FORM which follows. Your cash flow and net worth tell you where you are now, where you are headed, and provide the basis for dealing with changes you may want to make. REALITY is the key word here. With it you can project into the future with confidence and relief. Without it, you have only ambiguity and confusion.

Do not hide from the truth of the numbers. Here is a sample CASH FLOW FORM. Scan it briefly. An explanation of column headings is given below.

CASH FLOW FORM

	LAST 12 MONTHS	ESTIMATE NEXT 12 MONTHS	COMMENTS
SOURCES OF TAXABLE INCOME			
Employment Income--His	$ 37,085	_____	
Employment Income--Hers	25,000	_____	
Alimony	0	_____	
Pension--His	0	_____	
Pension--Hers	0	_____	
Social Security--His	0	_____	
Social Security--Hers	0	_____	
Dividends	0	_____	
Interest	533	_____	
Capital Gains	0	_____	
Taxable--Other	0	_____	
TOTAL TAXABLE INCOME	$ 62,618	_____	
NON-TAXABLE INCOME			
Child Support	0	_____	
Tax Free Municipal Bonds	0	_____	
Non Taxable--Other	0	_____	
TOTAL NON TAXABLE INCOME	0	_____	

	LAST 12 MONTHS	ESTIMATE NEXT 12 MONTHS	COMMENTS
TOTAL SOURCES OF INCOME	$ 62,618	_____	
TAXES			
Federal Income Taxes	$ 7,461	_____	
State Income Taxes	1,900	_____	
FICA Taxes	4,439	_____	
Other	0	_____	
TOTAL TAXES	$ 13,800	_____	
NET INCOME AFTER TAXES	$ 48,818	_____	
COMMITTED EXPENSES			
HOUSING			
Mortgage Payment	$ 8,664	_____	
Rent	0	_____	
Property Taxes	1,020	_____	
Homeowners Insurance	638	_____	
Utilities/Fuel	1,000	_____	
Maintenance/Repair	1,642	_____	
Other	0	_____	
TOTAL HOUSING	$ 12,964	_____	
TRANSPORTATION			
Auto Loan Payments	$ 4,128	_____	
Insurance	1,575	_____	
Gas/Oil/Repair	1,900	_____	
Other (commuting, etc.)	1,584	_____	
TOTAL TRANSPORTATION	$ 9,187	_____	
EDUCATION			
School and College	0	_____	
Other	0	_____	

	LAST 12 MONTHS	ESTIMATE NEXT 12 MONTHS	COMMENTS
TOTAL EDUCATION	0	_____	
INSURANCE			
Life	$ 473	_____	
Disability	0	_____	
Medical	0	_____	
Other	0	_____	
TOTAL INSURANCE	$ 473	_____	
OTHER COMMITTED EXPENSES			
Food	$ 3,100	_____	
Clothing/Cleaning	4,300	_____	
Phone	654	_____	
Personal Care	818	_____	
Medical Care	3,000	_____	
Prescription Drugs	235	_____	
Care for Dependents	0	_____	
Repayment of Loans/Charges	1,800	_____	
Business Meals & Travel	0	_____	
Tax-Deductible--Other	0	_____	
Non Tax-Deductible--Other	7,000	_____	
Alimony	0	_____	
TOTAL OTHER COMMITTED	$ 20,907	_____	
DISCRETIONARY EXPENSES			
Entertainment/Dining	$ 5,000	_____	
Vacation/Recreation/Club	6,000	_____	
Gifts	0	_____	
Hobbies	800	_____	
Home Improvements	0	_____	
Expenses for Long Term Goals	0	_____	
Miscellaneous Purchases	0	_____	
Tax-Deductible--Other	0	_____	

	LAST 12 MONTHS	ESTIMATE NEXT 12 MONTHS	COMMENTS
Non Tax-Deductible--Other	5,764	_____	
TOTAL DISCRETIONARY	$ 17,814	_____	
INVESTMENT OUTLAYS			
IRA	0	_____	
Keogh	0	_____	
Pension Plans	$ 3,537	_____	
Other Asset Purchases	0	_____	
TOTAL INVESTMENT OUTLAYS	$ 3,537	_____	
TOTAL EXPENSES	$ 78,682	_____	
NET CASH FLOW (negative)	($16,244)	_____	

EXPLANATION OF THE COLUMN HEADINGS

LAST 12 MONTHS

This refers to the last 12 months during which you were part of a couple and your income and expenses were combined. However, if you have lived alone a full 12 months, use those figures. Or 3f you lived alone for a shorter period and can extend to one year, that will work too. The objective is to have a 12 month base period during which your spending was fairly consistent.

ESTIMATED NEXT 12 MONTHS

It is easiest to fill out each item in this column immediately after you have completed calculating the same line for the last 12 months, while the figures are still fresh in your mind. Many items such as rent, mortgage and property taxes will remain the same if you do not move. However, others such as auto expenses, groceries, clothing and cleaning will change. You may be tempted to make some changes while you are estimating the next 12 months, but wait until you have read Chapter 5.

COMMENTS

Use this section to write down thoughts and reminders as you are collecting information. For example, you might note that you are going to be spending less or more in the next 12 months for a particular item, or that payments are coming up which did not occur in the last period.

Now it's time for you to complete your own CASH FLOW FORM. You will find a blank CASH FLOW FORM in the Appendix.

INCOME ITEMS

The income portion of your CASH FLOW FORM is divided into sections: taxable and non-taxable. This is done because you will need to estimate your income taxes as one of your expenses.

Probably the easiest place to get the income figures will be from your last tax return. Be sure to adjust the employment income for raises which have occurred.

Dividend and interest income can be taken from Schedule B on your tax return. You can also get the same information from your 1099's. If you think that interest rates will change this year, then adjust your estimates for the next 12 months accordingly. One way to accomplish this is to compare the rates paid last year to those being paid now. To get this information, just call the companies that sent the 1099's and ask them, or look in the business section of your newspaper. If, for example, last year you owned 90 day C.D.'s and they paid 10%, look to see what banks or savings and loans are paying for 90 day C.D.'s now.

If you have sold a piece of property or some other asset, the difference between your cost and the sales price should be entered in the capital gain section. Show the total amount of the gain here. If you still owe money on the asset that you have sold, and it must be paid within the next 12 months, put the total amount owed in the expense portion under "Non Tax-Deductible--Other."

For purposes of cash flow, show the net income you get from your rental properties after expenses, debt service and taxes on the building. Enter this rental net income in the section marked "Taxable--Other" income. Do not include depreciation as an expense since it is a non-cash item.

"Non Taxable--Other" income would include annual principal that is being paid back to you from a loan, life insurance proceeds, the principal from annuity contracts, or other transactions in which the principal has not increased.

TAXES

Use your tax return to enter last year's taxes. To estimate next year's taxes use the TAXABLE INCOME total from your CASH FLOW FORM and find your tax rate in the ranges shown below. Then multiply your income by the rate to obtain your estimated income tax. Note: these rates will change as the laws change.

TAXABLE INCOME	1988 TAX RATE
$5,000-17,850	15%
$17,850-$43,150	28%
$43,150 and up	33%

For example, if your taxable income is $40,000, then your tax would be $8,879 (15% of $17,850 plus 28% of $40,000-$17,850). So for purposes of figuring your cash flow you would enter $8,879 in the

"Federal Income Taxes" section. This very rough method does not account for federal deductions and exemptions, or, on the other side, for FICA and state taxes. It will not be accurate, but it will be close enough to help you get an idea of your cash flow. Enter this number on the "Total Taxes" line also since it is an estimate of all your taxes.

EXPENSES

The easiest way to trace your expenses is to go through your checkbook for the last 12 months. Use columnar paper and column headings from the CASH FLOW FORM. Enter each check under the appropriate column.

Cash is a source of leaks. Although you will not be able to account for how it is spent to the penny, you will find that there is a consistent pattern. Usually people take out the same amount of cash every week for things like lunches, allowances etc. Try to visualize how you spend and into which category of expenses the entries belong. If you see an unusually large amount of cash taken out, try to trace what it was used for. Often it will be for a vacation, a trip or to celebrate a major event.

Credit card charges need to be broken out by expense type also. Even though you pay the credit card companies separately, credit cards are not an expense. They are a method of financing your expenses. So it is necessary to separate the items and put them into the appropriate categories.

Add the totals from your checkbook, cash, and credit cards on your columnar paper and enter the totals on your CASH FLOW FORM in the column marked "Last 12 Months." Since you are actually listing the amounts of purchases charged on your credit cards in the appropriate category, it is important to remember not to include the money you send to the credit card companies as an expense. There will be a duplication of expenses if you do this.

Now estimate each of those expense items for the next 12 months accounting for any anticipated changes. Remember, don't make unwanted adjustments at this point.

NET CASH FLOW

After you have collected all your information and made your estimates just subtract total expenses from total income. The result is your cash flow. The figure could be positive or negative, and it could be wrong. Look at it for reasonableness. If, for example, your calculations show that your estimated net cash flow for the next 12 months will be significantly more positive than your last 12 months, you need to ask yourself "Why?" Or if any of the figures just "feel" wrong, reexamine your data.

Once you are satisfied that your financial reality is reasonably accurate, you are in a position to change it. First, however, you need to know what you want. You may think that is very clear to you right now--you want more money! Or, on the other hand, you may think you have plenty of money and simply want to know how to invest it. Before you take action to accomplish either of these goals, it is necessary to become more specific. The next chapter will help you do this.

CHAPTER 5

WHAT DO YOU WANT?

Figuring out what you want can be quite difficult if you have not yet accepted the fact that you are alone with your money. Since money was a part of your lost relationship, your feelings and opinions may still reflect that relationship.

Additionally, most of your life you have been getting messages about money. Money can be thought of rationally. It can be quantified. It can also be thought of emotionally. "If I had enough money, everything would be all right." When you ask almost anyone what she wants, the reply will be "you mean if I had unlimited money?" We encourage people to acquire money and then criticize them when they seem too acquisitive.

Once at a party I overheard three women roasting a fourth. It seemed that the one they were talking about was beautiful but poor, and she was dating a man who was unattractive and rich. They were accusing her of going out with him just because he had money. They did not mention that he might have been going out with her just because she was beautiful. Our culture tells us that it is acceptable to fall in love for beauty, but not for money. People do it anyway. Even if relationships start without money as a focal point, they end up affected by it. Attitudes develop which influence behavior, decision-making, and the relationship itself. Ask yourself the following questions and write down your answers. Although some of the questions may seem redundant, fill them all in anyway.

1. Who made the money decisions in your relationship?

2. Were you totally dependent on your mate to make money decisions?

3. Was your attitude one of "He earns the money; I spend it"?

4. Did he make money decisions without consulting you?

5. Did you like the way your mate handled money?

6. Are you holding on to an "if only"? "If only we had invested in that property when we had that chance." "If only he had got out of the stock market in time." "If only" this or that had happened.

7. Did you and your partner fight about money?

8. Did you spend money to feel better?

9. Did you stay together because of money?

10. Did you have enough money?

11. Did your mate admire the way you spent money?

12. Did he put you down for the way you handled money?

13. If your former partner were inside your head right now, what would he think about the way you are handling your money?

Think about this last question for a minute longer. After you come up with the answer say either aloud or to yourself one of the following:

"I'm glad you like and approve of how I am handling my money." It is important to me that I say 'good-by' to you now about money. I need to make my own decisions without taking you into account."

"I'm sorry you do not like the way I am handling my money. It is important to me that I say 'good-by' to you now about money. I need to make my own decisions without taking you into account."

So that you can accept your current financial reality, it is important that you say "good-by" to the money aspects of your past relationships. If you admired the way your spouse handled money, say either to yourself or aloud: "I admired the way you handled money; good-by to that part of our relationship." Or "I hated the way you handled money; "good-by to that part of our relationship." Saying "good-by" may be frightening but it is also freeing.

No longer do you have to take your mate into consideration when making money decisions. You are free to make your own.

No longer are you going to fight with him about money.

No longer do you need to accept his judgement about how you handle money.

It is no longer relevant that he screwed things up or that he was fabulously successful.

You are no longer in that relationship. The financial reality you discovered in the last chapter is yours. You can use it or abuse it. You are now free TO DO WHAT YOU WANT, and to do this successfully you must first identify what you want.

It does not work simply to say "I want to be happy." There is nothing wrong with this goal; it's just too vague. You need to be more specific.

The goals outlined in the following pages can be defined and quantified. They are facilitative in nature, and although they may help you be happier, they are not impulse wishes as discussed in Chapter 2. This is an important distinction because even if you reach the goals we talk about, you may not be happy. Remember Patty, who spent lots of money buying things but did not get the nurturing and the loving that she wanted.

Setting goals is a two step process. First you must identify them so that you really understand what you want. Then you will put them in the order of importance to you.

IDENTIFYING YOUR GOALS

The following are examples. Some may match your own; others will not. Pick and chose, but TELL THE TRUTH.

GOAL #1 DO YOU WANT MORE MONEY TO SPEND?

If this is one of your goals, how MUCH more do you want? Be very specific about answering this and express it in terms of amount per month. Before you write down how much, ask yourself what you will buy with the extra money. To figure this out, you should refer to the cash flow form you completed in the previous chapter. Ask yourself, "If I had more money, how would I spend it?" An example might be "$50 more per month for clothes." You really should not limit yourself here. There is plenty of time to cut back later. Exclude large purchases such as a new house or a car; these are separate goals.

GOAL #2 DO YOU WANT TO PLAN FOR RETIREMENT?

This means planning to make sure you have enough money to support yourself during your total retirement. Of course the big questions are "How much is enough?" and "How long will my retirement last?" The answers to these questions are not simple, and unless you are particularly adept with financial calculators, you should get some help from a professional financial planner. Included in Appendix B is a detailed description of how to calculate your retirement if you are so inclined.

GOAL #3   DO YOU WANT TO PLAN FOR YOUR CHILDREN'S EDUCATION?

If so, decide what school or college you would like them to attend. If they were to go to that school today, how much would it cost for one year? You can get this number by calling the college or school registrar. They will give you tuition plus typical living expenses. You will want to add other expenses depending on your perception of what is needed. Multiply this total by the number of years required and you will get the total education cost in today's dollars.

To find out what this cost is in tomorrow's dollars and to calculate how much you will need to save, earmark, borrow, or steal, either follow the procedure for calculating retirement as described in the appendix or seek some professional financial planning help.

GOAL #4 DO YOU WANT TO BUY SOME MAJOR ITEMS?

List those things you want to buy, when you want to buy them, and how much you estimate they will cost. "Major" would be something that you would ordinarily not put on a credit card, such as a new car or a house. Be specific. Do not be intimidated by the fact that you may not be able to pay for them in full at the time of purchase. Your future planning will help you decide how to finance them.

GOAL #5   DO YOU WANT TO BE SURE YOU HAVE THE RIGHT KIND OF INSURANCE COVERAGE?

This subject will be covered in detail in Chapter 7.

GOAL #6 DO YOU WANT TO BE FINANCIALLY SECURE?

Everyone wants enough money to be secure. But how do you

measure security and how much is enough for you?

HOW TO MEASURE YOUR SECURITY

Your net worth is a measure of your financial security. By dividing either your annual or monthly total expenses into your net worth figure, you discover how long this net worth will support your current expenses. For example, if your net worth is $300,000 and your monthly expenses are $4,000, then you have 75 months or 6.25 years of security ($300,000 divided by $4,000). You get the same answer on an annual basis by dividing your net worth by your annual expenses ($300,000 divided by $48,000 equals 6.25 years).

Unless you are willing to move from your present home, the above calculation, although accurate, can lead to a false sense of security. You should adjust for the equity in your house. In the example above, if $140,000 of your net worth was equity in your house, subtract $140,000 from the $300,000 net worth, leaving $160,000. Then divide that $160,000 by $4,000. So your "financial security" could be seen as 40 months or about 3.33 years. The point is that although certain items, like your home, have monetary value, they should be taken out of the calculation unless you would consider changing them. If you are planning a change, be sure to add any additional expenses beyond your mortgage payment. If you sell your house, you will have to live somewhere. If you decide to rent and your monthly rental is more than your current mortgage payment, add the difference to your total expenses.

HOW MUCH IS ENOUGH?

The answer depends on your ability to earn money, and your other sources of income. Most young people are not particularly concerned about financial security. They know intuitively that they have a long time to earn money. They may also believe that mom and dad will still help. As people grow older and more independent, they become aware of the need to be personally responsible for their own future security.

If you have very recently become "alone with your money," you probably think you need more financial security than you needed before. In fact, you may need less or the same amount. It is a function of your net worth, your expenses, and your other sources of income, such as income from your present job, parental support, child support, alimony, social security, or insurance.

In my experience, I find that most people would like more financial security than they have. They feel the most secure when they have a lot of cash or cash equivalents, and they are willing to give up current satisfaction for future security.

There is a dilemma here. If too much cash is held, then assets will not grow and your future can be less abundant. If not enough cash is held and everything is invested, then you are vulnerable to changes in economic conditions and unpredictable investment results. The solution is to create a balance between cash, or cash equivalents, and investments.

How much cash or cash equivalents is enough? Most people are comfortable with 3 to 6 months' living expenses. However, this amount is entirely a function of your "comfort level." When you are trying to quantify your financial security goal, you should express it in terms of number of months' expenses. Ask yourself the following questions before deciding on the actual number:

1. Is your job secure? If not, how long would it take you to find another?

2. Can you depend on your former mate to pay the alimony or child support? Is his job secure?

3. Do you need to invest your assets for growth to plan for retirement and other needs?

4. If your current source of income is cut off, how capable are you of creating another? For example, if you were to become disabled, would you have enough income to support yourself?

5. Do you need to have your assets earn more income than they do presently?

Actually write down the answers to these questions. You should arrive at a sense of how many months of "financial security" you would like and how that should be balanced against future income needs.

GOAL #7 DO YOU WANT TO BE SURE YOUR ESTATE PLAN IS IN ORDER?

First, you want to assure orderly distribution of your estate. If you do not have a will, your state will assume the responsibility for dividing up your estate. This will be time consuming and it may not be distributed as you would like. You can solve this problem with a written will, which you create by yourself or with an estate attorney. There are books available to show you how.

Next, you want to do what you can to eliminate or lower estate taxes and probate expenses. I recommend that you use an estate attorney. A certified financial planner can help also.

GOAL #8 DO YOU WANT TO LOWER YOUR TAXES?

Be careful with this one. It is very easy to get caught up in trying to avoid paying taxes to the government. The only reason to cut down on your taxes is so that you will have more money for yourself. Most of the horror stories you have heard about tax shelters occurred because people were preoccupied with avoiding taxes instead of making money.

GOAL #9 DO YOU WANT TO MAKE MORE MONEY ON YOUR ASSETS?

A need to increase the yield on your existing assets may seem to be a primary goal. However, it is only necessary if some of your other financial goals require it. If you have all the security you need, you do not need to increase the yield on your assets. Why bother, since increasing the yield generally increases the risk?   If the answer to this is simply that you like the idea of making money for yourself, the balance of this book will help by giving you the foundation you need to get started. You will, however, need to read other books on investing and/or get help from a financial planner.

GOAL #10 DO YOU HAVE A RELATIVE YOU WANT TO TAKE CARE OF?

Express this goal in dollars per month or year and put it in the Committed Expense portion of your CASH FLOW FORM under "Non Tax-Deductible Other" expenses.

QUANTIFYING YOUR GOALS

Unless you have sufficient funds to accomplish all of your goals, you must establish the relative importance of each one. To do this, first identify the importance of each goal on a scale from 0 to 10, with 10 being extremely important and 0 not very important to you at all. Then establish the relative importance of each; in other words, rank them. First, pick the most important goal; make that "A." If you have a couple of goals that you have given the same importance, select the most important. Then decide which is the least important of your goals and make that "I" (if you have 9 items, "J" if you had 10 etc.). Then pick the second most important goal and mark it "B" and the second least important and mark it "H." Do this until all your items are ranked.

SAMPLE GOAL EVALUATION

GOAL	HOW MUCH	WHEN	IMPOR-TANCE	RANK
Retirement	Not sure	2007	10	B
Children's Education	NA	Done	0	I
More Spendable Income	$1,000	Monthly	7	F
Buy a New Car	$15,000	1990	8	E
Financial Security	9 Months	Now	10	A
Estate Plan	NA	Now	6	G
Insurance	NA	Now	6	H
Reduce My Taxes	Minimal	1988	10	D
Take Care of Sick Mother	$1,000	Monthly	10	C

NA means not available or not applicable.

When this is done rearrange the order so that the most important goal is first.

SAMPLE GOALS RANKED

Rank	GOAL	HOW MUCH	WHEN
A.	Financial Security	9 Months	Now
B.	Retirement	Not Sure	2007
C.	Take Care of Sick Mother	$1,000	Monthly
D.	Reduce My Taxes	Minimal	Next Year
E.	Buy a New Car	$15,000	In 3 years
F.	More Spendable Income	$1,000	Monthly
G.	Estate Plan	NA	Now
H.	Insurance	NA	Now
I.	Children's Education	NA	Done

STOP! ! !

Before you go any further, sit down and do this goal setting for yourself. It is NOT a test. It does not have to be perfect, accurate, or reasonable the first time you try it. But I guarantee you that if you make a stab at it, do the best you can, rework it and rethink it (get help if you want), you will have a clearer picture of your own situation and needs. You can always change it. In fact you WILL change it. I encourage you to rethink your goals every few months as your life changes.

CHAPTER 6

WHAT TO DO WHEN THERE IS
NOT ENOUGH MONEY

I have had many clients who felt they did not have enough money. In all cases, the overall solutions called for obtaining more income, cutting expenses, or a combination of both. I have given the same kinds of advice to those people who eventually got what they wanted as I did to those who did not. People who were successful either had access to more income than was apparent originally, or were strongly motivated to change their spending habits. People who were unsuccessful were going to have to make some kind of sacrifice (often only temporary) and were unwilling to change. Or else they wanted something different from what they thought they did in the beginning.

June & Joy will be used as examples. Both clients had a limited amount of money and at the time they came to me were spending more than they were receiving.

Reducing expenses at the outset was going to be necessary in each case. The plan I did for Joy was immediately successful. June's was immediately unsuccessful. The difference between the two was that Joy's plan was designed for what she REALLY wanted to accomplish. June's plan was designed for what she SAID she wanted. The distinction is important and it is not always easy to discern the truth, as you will see. This chapter will show you how important it is to make that distinction. It will also give you specific suggestions on solving your money shortage problems.

JUNE

When June came to see me, she said "I want to control what I spend." She was worried about spending more than her income. She had divorced well, having received over $800,000 in assets and an alimony settlement of $5,000 a month. While married to Jason, the president of a Fortune 500 company, she had not had to think about controlling her expenses. It was as if the money she spent came from a spigot which never closed. So trying to control expenses was new to June. I felt she should have an additional goal: to protect her capital so that it could support her in case Jason became unable to pay the alimony. Corporate executives can lose their jobs more easily than one might think.

JUNE'S FINANCIAL REALITY

Half of June's net worth was in her house and in a condo that she owned and was renting to one of her children. Forty percent was in stock from the corporation for which her ex husband worked. The rest was in a note that was due in 3 years, on which $500 a month interest was being paid.

Her cash flow was a negative $1,000 a month. Although her mortgage payments were only $238 a month, her total housing expenses were about $1,000, or 20% of her income. She spent $500 a month on allowances for her children, $500 a month for taking care of horses, riding lessons and other ancillary costs, and about $1,000 a month on clothes, mostly for the children. Additionally, the condo that she rented to her son had an annual negative cash flow of about $1,000. She was spending over 50% of her total income on her children in one way or another.

JUNE'S PLAN

June had decided that she wanted to sell the stock she had received as a settlement. She was nervous about the stock market and she was nervous about the company Jason was running. By selling the stock she was going to have to pay about $80,000 in taxes and would be left with around $220,000 for investing.

She decided that she did not want to keep much of that money liquid; she was afraid she would spend it, and she wanted to position it for growth.

She also decided that she wanted to buy a house to restore and sell. She planned to rent the house to one of her other sons while she was remodelling it. She figured that she would need about $75,000 for the down payment and upgrading. She had enjoyed restoring the various houses that she and her family had lived in. The nature of Jason's career had caused the family to move many times; so she had considerable experience in making homes livable. Additionally, she thought she had located a bargain which, with a little fixing-up, could generate a tidy profit. I thought it was a good idea. The numbers seemed right, and so long as she held down her expenses and her son paid the rent, the plan would work.

Along with this, she was going to cut her expenses by $1,000 per month by getting rid of her daughter's horse, reducing the money spent for clothes by $300 a month and cutting their allowances by $200 a month.

This plan gave her a neutral cash flow, positioned her assets for growth, and protected her in the event that her ex-husband could not pay the alimony.

JUNE IMPLEMENTS HER PLAN

June was excited about her plan. She felt that she was on top of things and would accomplish her goals. This is how her implementation proceeded:

1. She immediately bought the fixer-upper and had her younger son (27 years old) move in. She put $50,000 down for the house, and fixed it up nicely with another $50,000 ($25,000 more than we had budgeted). The mortgage on the house was $1,000 a month. Her son and his housemate were to pay her

79

$1,000 a month and she would take care of all the other expenses. After 3 months, her son could not pay the rent. Instead of getting another tenant, June continued to let him live there for a full year without rent.

2. She could not bring herself to tell her daughter that the horse had to go. She continued spending the money for another year on the horse. Finally, when the daughter moved out and went to college, the horse was sold.

3. She had a talk with her daughters about cutting back their allowances and clothing expenses. Those changes were made.

4. Her situation worsened rather than improved. She thought that the problem was that she was having a hard time keeping track of her expenses. She hired somebody to help pay her bills and manage her money. Still she was using up her capital. Every month she would call to cash in some of her investments to meet her expenses. We met on a regular basis. I counselled her:

   a. Either insist that her son pay the $1,000 a month, get new tenants, or sell the house.

   b. Either insist that her other son pay $500 more a month for his condo, get new tenants, or sell the condo.

   c. If unwilling to do "a." and "b.", go to work to earn the supplemental income needed to keep from losing her capital.

5. One day she called to ask me what I thought about her daughter spending $15,000 for a horse that was a steal and which, with a little work, could be sold for a handsome profit. I asked her whether her daughter had $15,000 and she said "No " that she would have to lend it to her. I told her that if she wanted to buy the horse for her daughter, that was one thing,

but for investment purposes it was too risky for her. She insisted that it was a good business deal and bought the horse. Within six months, the horse had an accident and had to be killed.

6. Jason, in the meantime, lost his job. Because of a contractual obligation on the part of his company, he was still able to pay the alimony. However, these payments could stop at any moment.

June did not take my advice. She could not bring herself to disappoint her children. Her younger son, Eric, who lived in the fixer-upper, had a history of problems, and her older boy was a struggling song writer. She was particularly concerned about Eric and felt that if she helped one of her children she should help them all. As a parent, I certainly understood her dilemma. As a financial planner I became rather a thorn in her side as I continued to remind her of what she needed to do to keep from going broke.

People don't like to be told what they don't want to hear; so I didn't hear from her for eight months. When she called she said she had good news. Eric had gotten married and had a job as a real estate salesman. She had sold Eric's house and her own house and had bought two different houses in a less expensive part of town. One of the houses was going to be rented by Eric and his new wife for $1,000 a month. This would once again be enough to pay the mortgage. I tried to be supportive and pleased for her, but I was quite worried. Yes, she had sold the houses, but not to cut her expenses or to take care of herself. She was taking care of Eric again. He was going to get the commissions for the real estate transactions and he was still going to be renting from his mother. Three months later, Eric was out of the real estate business and once again could not pay his rent. June was back to square one.

What did June get from all this? She said that she was very close with her family. She was able to see her grandchildren whenever she wanted and she was in constant contact with all of her family members. Most of her activities revolved around them. When I

81

asked her if she thought that her family would not love her if she stopped supporting them, she said "No." She was confident of their love and desire to be with her. Nevertheless, she was unwilling, for whatever reason, to cut down on the money she was spending on them.

June is not an irresponsible person. She is very much aware that she is using up her money but she doesn't REALLY believe it will happen. Once I asked her, "Why, if you know you are using up your money, do you continue to do it." She said " I am an optimist, and I know that it will work out." She still believed that the spigot would not be turned off. I do not know what will happen to June. My guess is that she will have to get much closer to poverty before she decides to cut back in any meaningful way.

So long as she does not have the will to say "No" to her children she will be in the hole. Her children, who grew up getting everything they wanted, might have a difficult time adjusting, but they will survive. They might even be resentful for a while. But June will not lose them if the love is really there. If it is not, then she is better off finding that out while she still has enough money to take care of herself.

June spent a lot of money with me and other advisors trying to solve her problems. This money could have been saved if from the beginning we all had recognized that what she REALLY wanted was to support her children, even at her own jeopardy. If we had known that, there were other planning alternatives available to reduce her deficit spending.

JOY

When Joy asked me for help, she wanted to leave her husband (no children) but could not see how she would be able to live on her salary alone. She and her husband were barely making it on their combined salaries. The planning process we followed works, but the most important factor that made Joy's plan successful was

82

that she was strongly motivated. She was willing to change. Joy's answers were in the numbers, and if you are having money shortage problems, read her case. Although there is considerable detail, it is in this detail that solutions are found. The answers may not be the same for you, but the same type of analysis and thinking will help you find answers for yourself.

STEP 1 JOY'S CURRENT FINANCIAL REALITY

JOY'S AND DON'S NET WORTH STATEMENT

ASSETS	
Current Assets	$1,000
Residence	140,000
Investments	25,000
His IRA's	8,000
Her IRA's	10,000
His Pension Plan	96,000
Personal Belongings	35,000
TOTAL ASSETS	$315,000
LIABILITIES	
Home Mortgage	$60,000
Credit Cards	8,000
TOTAL LIABILITIES	$68,000
TOTAL NET WORTH	$247,000

JOY'S AND DON'S BEFORE DIVORCE CASH FLOW

	CURRENT ANNUAL	CURRENT MONTHLY	% OF GROSS INCOME
SOURCES OF INCOME			
TAXABLE			
Employment Income--His	$37,085	$3,090	59.2
Employment Income--Hers	25,000	2,083	39.9
Alimony	0	0	0
Pension--His	0	0	0
Pension--Hers	0	0	0
Social Security--His	0	0	0
Social Security--Hers	0	0	0
Dividends	533	44	9
Interest	0	0	0
Capital Gains	0	0	0
Taxable--Other	0	0	0
TOTAL TAXABLE INCOME	$62,618	$5,218	100.
NON TAXABLE INCOME			
Child Support	0	0	0
Tax Free Municipal Bonds	0	0	0
Non Taxable--Other	0	0	0
TOTAL INCOME	$62,618	$5,218	100.
TAXES			
Federal Income Taxes	$7,461	$621	11.92
State Income Taxes	1,900	158	3.03
FICA Taxes	4,439	369	7.09
Other	0	0	0
TOTAL TAXES	$13,800	$1,150	22.04
NET INCOME AFTER TAXES	$48,818	$4,068	79.3

	CURRENT ANNUAL	CURRENT MONTHLY	% OF GROSS INCOME
COMMITTED EXPENSES			
HOUSING			
Mortgage Payment	$8,664	$722	17.23
Rent	0	0	0
Property Taxes	1,020	85	1.63
Homeowners Insurance	638	53	1.02
Utilities and Fuel	1,000	83	1.60
Maintenance/Repair	1,642	136	2.62
Other			
TOTAL HOUSING	$12,964	$1,080	24.10
TRANSPORTATION			
Auto Loan Payments	$4,128	$344	6.59
Auto Insurance	1,575	131	2.52
Gas/ Oil/ Repair	1,900	158	3.03
Other (commuting, etc)	1,584	132	2.53
TOTAL TRANSPORTATION	$9,187	$765	14.67
EDUCATION			
School and College	0	0	0
Other Education	0	0	0
TOTAL EDUCATION	0	0	0
INSURANCE			
Life	$473	$39	76
Disability	0	0	0
Medical	0	0	0
Other	0	0	0
TOTAL INSURANCE	$473	$39	76
OTHER COMMITTED EXPENSES			
Food	$3,100	$258	4.6
Clothing/Cleaning	4,300	358	6.4

	CURRENT ANNUAL	CURRENT MONTHLY	% OF GROSS INCOME
Phone	654	55	1
Personal Care	818	68	1.2
Medical Care	3,000	250	4.4
Prescription Drugs	235	20	3
Care for Dependents	0	0	0
Repayment of Loans & Charges	1,800	150	2.7
Business Meals & Travel	0	0	0
Tax-deductible--Other	0	0	0
Non Tax-deductible--Other	7,000	583	10.4
Alimony	0	0	0
TOTAL OTHER COMMITTED	$20,907	$1,742	30.9
DISCRETIONARY EXPENSES			
Entertainment/Dining	$5,000	$417	7.4
Vacation/Recreation/Club	6,000	500	8.9
Other Gifts	0	0	0
Hobbies	800	67	1.2
Home Improvements	0	0	0
Expenses for Long Term Goals	0	0	0
Miscellaneous Purchase	0	0	0
Tax-deductible--Other	0	0	0
Non Tax-deductible--Other	5,764	480	8.5
TOTAL DISCRETIONARY	$17,814	$1,485	26.3
INVESTMENT OUTLAYS			
IRA	0	0	0
Keogh	0	0	0
Pension Plans	3,537	295	5.2
Other Asset Purchases	0	0	0
TOTAL INVESTMENT OUTLAYS	$3,537	$295	5.2
TOTAL EXPENSES	$64,882	$5,406	103.6
NET CASH FLOW (negative)	($2,264)	($188)	(3.6)

Joy's primary goal was to get out of her marriage with Don. She needed to figure out how she could live on her salary alone and she wanted to avoid a fight.

Her BEFORE DIVORCE CASH FLOW told us the following:

1. Housing expenses were about 21% of their gross income. Mortgage lenders look for housing expenses to be under 35%. So we needed to look elsewhere for excess spending and potential reductions to resolve the negative cash flow.

2. They owned two cars. One was older and paid for; the other was new and was being paid off at around $4,000 a year for the next four years. Their automobile payments were just about half what their mortgage payments were and their total transportation costs were running around 15% a year. Although this was on the high side, it was not too far out of line.

3. Their cash flow showed that expenses were $16,444 more than their income, almost 26% more. To finance this, ten thousand dollars had been taken from savings, and credit cards were used for the rest. Their NET WORTH STATEMENT showed their credit card liability was $8,000. They had to pay $150 minimum a month to the credit card companies. This shows on their CASH FLOW FORM under repayment of loans and charges because the past debt of $8,000 needed to be paid off.

4. Joy had spent $3,000 that year for cosmetic surgery which was not covered by insurance. Don had bought a new boat for $7,000. Neither of these expenses would be present when Joy became single; so they could be eliminated in budgeting Joy's expenses.

5. Their vacation/recreation expenses were around 10% of gross income. This was on the high side and was an area that could be reduced.

6. Their entertainment/dining expenses were about 8% of gross income, and this too was an area that could be cut back.

STEP TWO ANALYZING AND PRIORITIZING

The next thing we did was to explore her options by analyzing and setting priorities.

First we revised Joy's cash flow using only her own income as a basis but retaining the same before divorce expense ratios. To do this, we established her new total gross income and worked backward from the right hand "percent" column. Each percentage figure was multiplied by her new income figure to obtain the dollars she would require for each expense. In other words, we prorated her expenses to her new income. We eliminated the ratios representing the new boat and the cosmetic surgery.

JOY'S PRORATED CASH FLOW AFTER DIVORCE

	ANNUAL	MONTHLY	% OF GROSS (RATIOS)
SOURCES OF INCOME			
Employment--His	0	0	0
Employment--Hers	$25,000	$2,083	100.
Alimony	0	0	0
Pension--His	0	0	0
Pension--Hers	0	0	0
Social Security--His	0	0	0
Dividends	0	0	0
Interest	0	0	0
Capital Gains	0	0	0
Taxable--Other	0	0	0
TOTAL TAXABLE INCOME	$25,000	$2,083	100.

	ANNUAL	MONTHLY	% OF GROSS (RATIOS)
NON-TAXABLE INCOME			
Child Support	0	0	0
Tax Free Municipal Bonds	0	0	0
Non Taxable--Other	0	0	0
TOTAL NON TAXABLE	0	0	0
TOTAL SOURCES OF INCOME	$25,000	$2,083	100.
TAXES			
Federal Income Taxes	$3,050	$254	11.92
State Income Taxes	758	63	3.03
FICA Taxes	1,772	147	7.09
Other	0	0	0
TOTAL TAXES	5,581	465	22.04
NET INCOME AFTER TAXES	$19,419	$1,618	79.3
COMMITTED EXPENSES			
HOUSING			
Mortgage Payment	$3,459	$288	11.92
Rent	0	0	0
Property Taxes	407	33	1.63
Homeowners Insurance	255	21	1.02
Utilities/Fuel	399	33	1.60
Maintenance/Repair	656	54	2.62
Other	0	0	0
TOTAL HOUSING	$5,176	$431	20.70
TRANSPORTATION			
Auto Loan Payments	$1,648	$137	6.59
Insurance	629	52	2.52
Gas/Oil/Repair	759	63	3.03
Other (commuting, etc)	632	52	2.53

	ANNUAL	MONTHLY	% OF GROSS (RATIOS)
TOTAL TRANSPORTATION	$3,668	$305	14.67
EDUCATION			
School and College	0	0	0
Other	0	0	0
TOTAL EDUCATION	0	0	0
INSURANCE			
Life	$189	$15	76
Disability	0	0	0
Medical	0	0	0
TOTAL INSURANCE	$189	$15	76
OTHER COMMITTED EXPENSES			
Food	$1,238	$103	4.6
Clothing/Cleaning	1,717	143	6.4
Phone	327	27	1
Personal Care	327	27	1.2
Medical Care	0	0	0
Prescription Drugs	94	7	3
Care for Dependents	0	0	0
Repayment of Loans & Charges	719	59	2.7
Business Meals/Travel	0	0	0
Tax-Deductible--Other	0	0	0
Non Tax-Deductible--Other	0	0	0
Alimony	0	0	0
TOTAL OTHER COMMITTED	$4,335	$362	17.3
DISCRETIONARY EXPENSES			
Entertainment Dining	$1,996	$166	7.4
Vacation/Recreation/Club	2,395	199	8.9
Charitable Contributions	100	8	4
Other Gifts	0	0	0
Hobbies	319	26	1.2

	ANNUAL	MONTHLY	% OF GROSS (RATIOS)
Home Improvements	0	0	0
Expenses for Long Term Goals	0	0	0
Miscellaneous Purchase	0	0	0
Tax-Deductible--Other	0	0	0
Non Tax-Deductible--Other	2,301	191	8.5
TOTAL DISCRETIONARY	$7,112	$592	26.3
INVESTMENT OUTLAYS			
IRA	0	0	0
Pension Plans	1,412	117	5.2
TOTAL INVESTMENT OUTLAYS	$1,412	$117	5.2
TOTAL EXPENSES	$27,493	$2,291	110.0
NET CASH FLOW (negative)	$(2,493)	$(207)	(10.0%)

As Joy went through the first two steps, she realized that there were some things that were more important to her than others. She also knew that some of the prorated expenses were unrealistic, but she could use them as a guide. Here are some of the things she learned from the above numbers.

1. If she continued to spend as she and Don had been spending, she would have a negative cash flow of approximately $2,500 a year. Since she did not want a negative cash flow and could see no other sources of revenue, she was going to have to reduce her spending in some way.

2. The total she could spend on housing was $431 a month. The mortgage alone was $722 a month. Either the house would have to be sold, she would have to move, or she would need help paying for it.

91

3. The total she could spend for transportation was $305 a month, including payment for a car, gas, oil, and insurance. As a couple, their car payments were $344 a month. The only way she could keep that new car was if it were paid off. They did not have the money to pay it off.

4. She had no dependents; so she needed no life insurance. The prorated schedule had her paying $15 a month for life insurance.

5. Her prorated food schedule was $103 a month or $23 a week. She wanted to lose weight, but not that much. This meant she would be spending more for food than the prorated schedule outlined.

6. She was quite upset by how much the schedule told her she could spend on clothes and cleaning. She wanted to adjust this upward somehow, even if it meant giving up something else.

7. The prorated amount for personal care was also unrealistically low. It showed $27 a month. A manicure now cost $40 a month. Having her nails and hair done was extremely important to her. She wanted to be able to spend more on this category.

8. The monthly payments to the credit card company could be eliminated through the property settlement. That was one expense she did not need.

9. Temporarily she would not be giving money to charities; so that $100 could be eliminated.

10. The allocation of $1412 annually for the pension plan would be changed to IRA contributions. She wanted to increase this to $2,000.

11. The category called "Non-Deductible--Other" was very high. This represented cash that she and Don used to spend. She

felt that she could bring this expense down by paying attention to it.

At this point she knew she would have to control her money. So the next step was to establish priorities for her expenses. The prorated cash flow schedule worked only as a guideline; now she needed to arrive at real budget numbers.

To do this she listed her most important expense first and the least important last, then next most important and next least important until she had given priorities to all of her expenses. Here is a portion of her list:

JOY'S LIST OF PRIORITIES

RANK	ITEM
1.	Housing
2.	Utilities
3.	Food
4.	Auto Payment
5.	Personal Care
6.	Insurance—Auto
7.	Gas,Oil,Repair
8.	Phone
9.	Clothing/Cleaning
10.	Entertainment/Dining
11.	Medical Care/Insurance
12.	Vacation/Recreation
13.	IRA
14.	Gifts

When YOU go through this process, be honest with yourself. You will spend your money on those items which are truly of value to you anyway; so you may as well admit to these from the beginning rather than ranking them the way you think some sensible person should. In Joy's case, for example, personal care, phone and clothing all came before medical care and insurance. As a

93

financial planner, I would have put medical care before those items. But Joy was about to enter the singles scene and she knew what was important to her. As it turned out, clothing and cleaning should have been even higher on her list.

STEP 3 JOY'S PLAN

Joy had made it clear to me that she was not going to be able to earn much more money than she was currently making. She knew she was unwilling to break up with her husband and look for a new job at the same time and she felt that she would not want to work two jobs for a while.

There were no assets that would provide additional income. If she and Don sold the house, the equity could have been invested for income, but neither of them wanted to do that. Both would have had the problem of finding alternative housing. Besides, Don felt very strongly about keeping the house. He had let Joy know that he was ready to fight for it. He also had told her that there was no way she was going to get any of the pension money. His first wife had "done" that to him and he wasn't going to let it happen again. Since no more income was available, she would definitely need to lower her expenses.

Housing was her first priority. So she started by figuring out how much she could spend on a place to live. If she did manage to get the house in the settlement, her housing expense would be about $13,000 a year. This represented 52% of her income and was way out of proportion. If she kept the house, she would either have to have a roommate or earn substantially more money. She said she did not want a roommate. She would have to move.

This was a tough decision because she loved her house. However, when I asked her what she loved about it, her answer was that she liked her paintings and the other things she had which made it comfortable. She realized that she could create the same ambiance elsewhere.

This realization, plus the fact that Don wanted the house very much, made it easier for her to make a decision to move. Ironically, when she moved she ended up with two roommates; so perhaps it was really the fight about the house and full responsibility for it that she did not want. The next question was "How much could she spend for another place to live?" Her prorated cash flow schedule showed that she could spend about $5,175 a year, or $430 a month for rent. She shopped around and found that she could find a satisfactory living arrangement for this amount. So for a housing expense figure she left the $5,175.

Her second priority was auto payment. She loved the car that she and Don had bought. It was new, had a lot of frills and made her feel good when she drove it. If she kept the car, her auto payments would have been $344 a month, or 17% of her total income, which was about 2 & 1/2 times the percentage that she and Don were currently paying. To keep her new expenses in line with her old ones, she could afford to pay approximately $137 a month. This kind of payment meant that she could afford to borrow about $5,000 for a car. The new car she and Don owned cost around $20,000; so she would have had to come up with $15,000 and finance the rest in order to buy the same car. The money was not there. She could not afford the kind of car that she was used to driving unless it was paid for.

Their second car was relatively new, but it was rather dumpy, with no pizazz and no frills. Joy hated it. It did, however, have one advantage; it was free and clear. This was a tough decision for her but she needed transportation and she wanted out of the relationship. If she took the older car, her auto payments would be cut to zero and she would have more money for other things. She also knew that eventually she would have more money and could buy another car. She was sure Don would not object to keeping the good car; so she put down "0" for auto payments in her plan.

After working out these two major problems, she was able to fill in the rest of the figures to establish a budget. Some of the expenses, such as personal care, would be more than the original prorated figures showed; others would be less.

To arrive at her completed budget, we started with her net income. We did not include taxes in her priority ranking because she had no choice but to pay them. The objective of the ranking technique is to reduce or eliminate those expenses which are on the bottom of the list.

Here is what some of her planned expenditures looked like. The annual income remaining is after taxes.

JOY'S LIST OF PRIORITIES

RANK	ITEM	ANNUAL	MONTHLY	ANNUAL INCOME REMAINING
	Beginning Balance (net after tax)			$20,328
1.	Housing	$5,100	$425	$15,228
2.	Utilities	600	50	14,628
3.	Food	1800	150	12,828
4.	Auto Payment	0	0	12,828
5.	Personal Care	1,000	83	11,828
6.	Insurance-Auto	600	50	11,228
7.	Gas,Oil,Repair	900	75	10,328
8.	Phone	360	30	9,968
9.	Clothing Cleaning	2,000	167	7,968
10.	Entertainment Dining	1,200	100	6,768
11.	Med. Care	0	0	6,768
12.	Vacation/Recreation	1,500	125	5,268
13.	IRA	2,000	167	3,268
14.	Gifts	200	17	3,068
	Ending Balance			$3,068

Medical care, which should be on the top of the list, was not a priority because it was covered through her employer's group insurance. Since all of her priorities were covered it looked as if Joy could make it on her own with a $3,000 cushion. However, in order for the plan to work, Don had to agree to the following:

1. He would keep the house.

2. He would pay Joy's share of the community property out of the pension plan. The alternative was to sell the house, since there was no cash.

3. He would accept the liability of the credit cards in exchange for Joy's reducing her share of the pension plan.

4. He would take the new car and give Joy the old one.

STEP 4 JOY IMPLEMENTS THE PLAN

When Joy finished her plan, she knew that she could survive alone. She would not have some of the things that she had before, but she would be free.

Instead of talking directly to Don, she wrote him a letter outlining all of the above. Within two weeks Don had agreed to the settlement and Joy had moved out of the house. Although there were some tense moments, Don and Joy were able to work out their agreement without a major fight.

Joy still feels as if she does not have enough money and security, but she is happier than she had been for years.

STEP 5 JOY MAINTAINS THE PLAN

On paper, Joy's plan was sound. However, things did not work out exactly as she had hoped. After the first month she was in the hole

97

and did not understand why. She had some resistance to looking at the actual figures, but when she did, she could see what went wrong. She now summarizes every month. Things are very tight for her, and as long as they are she will need to keep track of her expenses and manage them. By doing this, she will continue to stay financially healthy.

In both Joy's and June's cases the financial planning answers to not having enough money could be found by using the five step process outlined below. If you are in a similar situation, I recommend that you approach it in this systematic way:

STEP 1 IDENTIFY YOUR CURRENT REALITY AND WHAT YOU WANT.

To do this, first calculate your net worth and your cash flow as outlined in Chapter 4. Then determine what you want. Remember, don't limit yourself here. There is plenty of time for that later. Since money only facilitates your aliveness, it is important to make sure that the way you are spending it is contributing to your life in positive and basic ways.

For example, if your washing machine continually breaks down and you are forced to wash everything by hand, a new machine might facilitate your aliveness by giving you more time to play, go to school, or relax. But you might really get satisfaction out of washing your clothes by hand. In this case, a new machine would not facilitate your aliveness. We talked about aliveness and your impulse wishes in Chapter 2. It is especially important not to let anyone else tell you what you want. If you have difficulty in this area, get some help. Psychologists can be especially helpful. I also highly recommend the Technologies For Creating program as a powerful tool for identifying what is important to you.

STEP 2 ANALYZE AND ESTABLISH PRIORITIES

Using your CASH FLOW FORM, first determine what percent each expense item represents of your total gross income. Identify any items that are particularly high or low. Change anything that will change automatically by virtue of your being single. Then rank your expenditures. Do this by listing the most important first and the least last and then the next most important and the next least important, until your list is complete. The ranking will not be difficult if you have completed STEP 1 above.

STEP 3 CREATE A PLAN

Now identify your options and actually write down what you plan to do. Is there any more income available? Can you earn more? Can you reposition your assets for income; that is, do you have some growth assets that should be sold and the money used to buy income producing investments? Is the house you live in too expensive for your income? Can you take in a house-mate, or should you sell the house and move into something more affordable? Are your expense ratios reasonable? Examine with a critical eye any expense ratio that is over 10%. Finally, create a budget based on your prorated and adjusted CASH FLOW FORM.

STEP 4 IMPLEMENT YOUR PLAN

Before you start implementing your plan, take a look at it and ask yourself this question: "Am I willing to do what I have outlined?" If you are, then say to yourself, "I am choosing to implement this plan." This is different from "having to" or thinking somebody (your former mate, for example) is making you do it. It doesn't matter whose fault it is that you are having to make these sacrifices. It only matters that you want to change your life and that you are choosing to do what is necessary to be responsible for yourself. If you don't, your plan will not work, no matter how good it is. If, instead, you choose to believe that someone will come along on a white horse, I wish you luck; you'll need it.

STEP 5 MAINTAIN YOUR PLAN

Keep track of your expenses and income and stay within your proposed cash flow budget. If you spend too much in one area, reduce another. There are two reasons for doing this. One is to make sure you remain financially secure. The other is to recognize your success and give yourself credit for your accomplishments.

SUMMARY CHECK LIST

1. Use the five step process outlined above.

2. Make sure that your assets are positioned to provide income if you need it.

3. Check the following leaks:

    a. Cash. If you are short of money, keep track of how you spend your cash. It is very easy to forget small amounts, which add up.

    b. Insurance. In the next chapter you will learn about insurance, what you need and what you do not need. You might be spending more on it than is necessary.

    c. Subscriptions. Are you automatically subscribing to things that you no longer use?

    d. Gifts. Are you spending too much on other people because you think you should? Sometimes buying things for other people is an excuse just to buy something. This can happen if you don't feel justified spending money on yourself but do feel it is O.K. to spend on others. The financial result is the same!

    e. Children. They can nickel and dime you out of dollars. Be careful of trying to compensate for their loss.

4. Be careful about acquiring a new spouse in order to solve your financial problems. If you are lucky enough to marry somebody with money and that person can enhance your aliveness, congratulations. It is dangerous, however, to let money become the major objective in seeking a mate. This can interfere with your judgement on the other qualities, such as compassion, sensitivity, and openness, that enhance a relationship. So although it is possible to end up financially secure, your aliveness can be thwarted. Create your own money solutions first and get a mate second.

5. Make sure your large expenses are not out of line. Keep your housing expense under 35% (preferably around 20%) and your transportation under 17% of your total gross income.

6. Keep track of your cash flow. This will help you stay conscious of your goals and assure that you are getting what you want from the money you do have.

7. Before buying things, ask yourself whether what you are about to buy will facilitate your aliveness. If it won't, don't buy it.

8. Explore the possibilities of finding actions you can take to increase your income, such as a second job, a new job, a house-mate.

9. If you feel overwhelmed in this process, get professional help. I'll discuss how to do that later. Your local library and book store also have information.

10. Remember, the financial answers are in the numbers, but real solutions will come only after you have chosen to do something about them.

11. One thing that you must do is accept your current reality. This does not mean that you have to accept it forever. When you know what that reality is, you can then decide how you want it to be. Once you have made this decision, if you are patient

and persistent, what you have will begin to change and move closer to what you want.

Now that you understand your financial reality and have set your goals, you have the foundation for making other financial decisions with some self-confidence. The next few chapters will expand your knowledge so you can make intelligent judgements about insurance, investments, and professional advisors.

CHAPTER SEVEN

WHAT YOU NEED TO KNOW ABOUT INSURANCE

The trouble with insurance is that its value is only recognized when some kind of catastrophe occurs. You can really appreciate this if you have ever had an insurance policy pay off. As a basis for financial security, insurance is the cheapest thing you can buy. However, it seems expensive because you rarely see a result. The money you spend does not provide tangible objects. Americans spend an average of $3,000 a year for insurance. You may need more or less than this, but if you are like most insurance customers, you are confused by what is available. This chapter will clear up some of that confusion and help you to buy insurance intelligently.

LIFE INSURANCE

Life insurance is a misnomer. It should be called "death insurance." After all, the only time it pays is when somebody dies.

Do you need it? The answer is "No." Only your dependents need it. You might WANT to buy life insurance to help pay the taxes on your estate, or to leave an estate, or for any of the other reasons that the insurance industry suggests, but it is really only needed by a dependent who depends on you for income. It is particularly important for you to remember this now that you are alone with your money. The money you spend on life insurance is not for you and YOU may need the money.

You should remember that, as with other investments, there is no free lunch with insurance. Promises of no premium payments after a certain time, having the ability to borrow out cash on a tax-free basis, and the building up of cash value are all features that are available from various life insurance policies. But they are not free!

Somehow, you will pay for them.

The two underlying variables that actuaries (the people who set insurance rates based on risk evaluation) take into consideration when establishing premiums for life insurance are age and health. So no matter when you buy life insurance, the cost of it will go up as you get older. Whether you pay this increasing cost directly or indirectly depends on the kind of life insurance policy you buy.

Annual renewable term life insurance reflects the cost of insurance directly. Every year the out-of-pocket premium goes up. At younger ages, this insurance is by far the cheapest. However, as you get older the out-of-pocket expense becomes quite high. If you buy this insurance, insist that it be guaranteed renewable. If it is not, the company could cancel your policy at the end of any year. The insurance industry categorizes annual renewable term as temporary insurance, as compared to whole life or permanent insurance.

Whole life insurance is considered permanent because the amount of cash you pay out of your pocket does not change, and once you have the insurance, you never have to qualify for it again. As in the annual renewable term policy, every year the premium goes up. However, the money to pay the increase comes from inside the policy. This is money that you have paid in excess premiums which has accumulated in an account called cash value. This account has been earning interest. Though your out-of-pocket cost may not change, the premium always goes up.

If your out-of-pocket cash expense never goes up with permanent insurance and it does with annual renewable term, why would you buy annual renewable term? A case study best illustrates the reason.

Betty, who is 35 and alone with her money, has two children ages 12 and 13. She owns very few assets except her house, which has a $100,000 mortgage. She has figured out that to cover the mortgage and her children's college educations and living expenses she needs $300,000 worth of life insurance. Although she is managing to support her family, money is always tight. The figures listed below show Betty's cost for $300,000 worth of term insurance versus $300,000 of universal life, a type of whole life insurance.

COMPARISON OF TERM VERSUS WHOLE LIFE FOR BETTY AGE 35
FACE VALUE OF POLICY $300,000

YEAR	TERM PREMIUM	TERM CUMULATIVE PREMIUM	WHOLE LIFE PREMIUM	WHOLE LIFE CUMULATIVE PREMIUM	DIFFER-ENCE
1	279	279	1,551	1551	1,272
2	282	561	1,551	3,102	2,541
3	282	843	1,551	4,653	3,810
4	285	1,128	1,551	6,204	5,084
5	291	1,419	1,551	7,755	6,344
6	474	1,893	1,551	9,306	7,413
7	516	2,409	1,551	10,857	8,448
8	555	2,964	1,551	12,408	9,444
9	597	3,561	1,551	13,959	10,398
10	660	4,221	1,551	15,510	11,289
11	729	4,950	1,551	17,064	12,111
12	798	5,748	1,551	18,612	12,864
13	876	6,624	1,551	20,163	13,539
14	981	7,605	1,551	21,714	14,109
15	1,071	8,676	1,551	23,265	14,589
16	1,173	9,849	1,551	24,816	14,967
17	1,281	11,130	1,551	26,367	15,237
18	1,416	12,546	1,551	27,918	15,372
19	1,563	14,109	1,551	29,469	15,360
20	1,725	15,834	1,551	31,020	15,186

These figures show that over the 20 year period, Betty will save approximately $15,000 in premiums by buying term versus whole life. In the 19th year, her term premium is more than the whole life policy premium. By this time, Betty's need for insurance may have diminished since her children will be finished with school and she anticipates her assets will have increased. The main advantage to Betty of the term policy is that she can get substantial coverage for much less money than she can with the whole life policy during a time in her life when money is very tight.

At this point you probably are wondering why anybody would buy anything but term life insurance. Some people buy whole life products because they like the "forced savings" aspect of it. The savings comes from paying excess premiums at early ages. From my perspective as a financial planner, I would rather see people buy term and invest the difference. But if you lack discipline and know you will not save, buying a whole life type of insurance product is one way to do it.

Universal life is one type of whole life policy that has some advantages people have found attractive. It is a product which allows you to increase or decrease the premium you pay as your needs change. When you do this you can increase or decrease the savings portion of the premium. You can increase or decrease the amount of insurance you have also. However, if you increase it substantially, the insurance company will require another medical examination. If you want, you can borrow money from your policy on a tax-free basis (this could change at any time depending on the mood of congress). The interest that is earned on your savings inside a whole life policy will change with the market for interest rates. Thus, when interest rates are going up, you will have a chance to earn more, and vice versa. Most of these policies have a guarantee of 4%. All interest that is earned inside universal life insurance and other insurance products is tax-free unless the policy is cancelled. When this happens, all the cash build-up inside the policy is taxed.

Another variety of whole life insurance is single premium whole life. With this kind of insurance, one premium is paid when the policy is purchased and no further out-of-pocket premiums are paid. This premium is substantially more than the actual cost of insurance for the first year. The excess premium earns interest inside the policy. All future annual costs of the life insurance are taken out of the build-up of earnings inside the policy. This kind of policy was very popular in the late 1980's for people who had substantial cash sitting in C.D.'s. Insurance companies were paying a higher interest rate than banks, and the interest was earned on a tax free-basis. The money could be borrowed out of the policy and, because it was a loan, no taxes were paid. This was considered a major tax break and as this book is being written, congress is considering legislation which would eliminate the tax advantages of this kind of policy.

WHICH KIND OF INSURANCE SHOULD YOU BUY

This decision depends on what you want to accomplish. If you are looking for the least expensive, you should buy annual renewable term. Every 4 or 5 years examine your needs to see whether you should change your insurance carrier. Rates vary from company to company, competition is fairly fierce and changing can create a savings. You also should consider switching to permanent insurance when you pass age fifty.

If you want to have permanent insurance and do not want to have to worry about increasing your out-of-pocket expenditures, universal life makes sense.

If your object is simply to deposit cash some place where the money earns on a tax-free basis, single premium whole life works.

HOW MUCH LIFE INSURANCE SHOULD YOU BUY?

One rule of thumb is to buy only as much as your dependents will need. This is logical and obvious, but since life insurance is purchased to take care of loved ones, emotion can interfere with judgement. I suggest quantifying your needs as described below: To protect your dependents with life insurance on your life, buy enough to pay off the major expenses, such as your mortgage and children's education, plus some to generate income. In Betty's case her mortgage was $100,000 and the estimated total expenses for her children's education was $50,000. To this we added $150,000 for living expenses. At the time she purchased the policy 6% interest could easily have been earned (assuming the benefit were paid to her heirs and put in a conservative investment) and 6% of $150,000 would generate about $750 taxable per month. Now she felt that she had covered her children's needs, given her ability to pay for insurance. She would have liked to buy more, but could not really afford the cash drain.

When buying life insurance for estate tax purposes, have your estate taxes calculated. For example, Betty's taxable estate (assets minus liabilities and estimated death expenses) is $400,000. This includes the insurance proceeds and the equity in her house. Because the federal government allows a $600,000 exclusion, there would be no estate taxes. Even after 20 years and assuming a 3.5% growth on her non-insurance assets, her total estate would be worth less than $500,000. So Betty's heirs will not have to pay estate taxes.

On the other hand, because Jean had "divorced well" and done an excellent job of managing her assets, her heirs will have an estate tax problem. Her half of the settlement was worth $1,200,000. Over a 10 year period these assets had grown to $2,200,000. The estate taxes on this will be approximately $345,800. Jean was worried about her heirs' having to pay so much money to the government. A significant amount of her assets were in real estate and were not liquid. She did not want them to have to sell at distressed prices and she did not like the idea of giving so much of her hard-earned money to the government in any case.

She was faced with a further dilemma. If she funded the taxes with insurance, the insurance proceeds would also be taxed. Her answer was to buy enough insurance to cover the taxes through the use of an insurance trust. Since the trust owned the policy and trusts don't die, the proceeds would not be taxable. This is a rather sophisticated estate planning technique and should never be attempted without professional help. In fact, you should never buy insurance for estate tax purposes without consulting an estate attorney or qualified financial planner. In addition to helping you make sure the insurance you are considering is correct for what you want to accomplish, these people may be able to show you ways to reduce your estate taxes without buying insurance.

You may find that as you get older and accumulate assets, you will become more self-insured and your need for life insurance will decrease. This is not true, however, of disability insurance.

DISABILITY INSURANCE

Betty needs disability insurance; Jean does not. Betty and her family are dependent on her income, whereas Jean lives on the income from her assets. Although social security would pay disability, Betty decided she wanted to buy disability insurance to provide more protection.

THINGS YOU NEED TO KNOW ABOUT DISABILITY INSURANCE

Although many legitimate insurers sell by mail or phone, fly-by-night insurers thrive on this kind of business. One way to protect yourself is to buy only from insurers who are licensed in your state.

A non-cancellable policy is more desirable than a guaranteed policy, but it is also more expensive. Furthermore, the language is confusing. A non-cancellable policy is one in which the policy will be renewed at a guaranteed rate up to a certain age. In other words, the premium cannot be changed. A policy that is only guaranteed is also guaranteed renewable up to a certain age, but the premium can be changed if the insurer changes the premium for your class of insureds.

Make sure the disability policy you buy has residual benefits. If you become disabled, but can still work, residual benefits will be paid if you earn less than 80% of what you earned before. You do not have to work in the same occupation as you did prior to your disability. Let's assume that Betty owns a disability income policy which will pay $2,400 a month. She becomes disabled. After three months she takes a job paying $1,600 a month. Prior to becoming disabled she earned $3,000. Because her policy has a residual benefit, she could still collect $1,120 (there is a formula for figuring this out) from the insurance company. This is a good deal for her because she is getting a total of $2,720 instead of the $2400 the insurance would pay if she did not work. It is also a good deal for the insurance company because instead of paying $2400 they are paying $1,120.

Make sure the policy pays for losses due to "accidental bodily injury" as opposed to "accidental means." The distinction is important. An injury caused by "accidental means" requires the injury to result from CAUSES which are accidental. For example if you develop a back injury while carrying something heavy, an "accidental means" policy would not cover the injury, because you were carrying the object intentionally. It would only be covered if you slipped while carrying the object and that accident caused your injury. On the other hand, a policy which covers "accidental bodily injury" would cover the injury.

When you buy a policy you will have to make a decision about how long you are willing to wait before receiving payments. Most people buy policies with 90 day waiting periods because they are less expensive than policies with shorter waiting periods. To whatever elimination period you choose, add 30 days because it will take that long to get your first check. Your decision needs to be based on your ability to support yourself during the time you would not be getting insurance money.

It would be better to buy disability insurance which paid off for life. However, lifetime policies are more expensive than policies which pay to age 65, and for that reason most people buy the latter. This means that if your disability persists after age 65, you will not be covered. If eligible you will, however, be able to get social security at that time. Contact your local social security office to learn what the eligibility requirements are.

When you buy disability insurance, the company will check into your medical background before approving the policy, but once the insurance has been issued, you will not have to be examined again.

MEDICAL INSURANCE

Because Betty works for a company that has group medical insurance, she and her family are protected. Jean, on the other hand, does not work and needs coverage. If you have no coverage, you should get some immediately; a major illness or accident could wipe out you and your family.

If your former spouse was covered by a group insurance policy, call his company's personnel department to see if you are eligible for continued coverage and if so, what you need to do to make that happen. If the company had 20 or more employees the COBRA laws provide that widowed or divorced dependents may continue their group benefits for specified periods after death or divorce. You must pay the premium of course, but at least you will be covered and there is a good chance that it will be lower than if you purchased the insurance on your own.

THINGS YOU NEED TO KNOW ABOUT MEDICAL INSURANCE

As with disability insurance, medical insurance should be purchased only from state licensed carriers.

It can be bought from a health maintenance organization (HMO) in which health expenses are pre-paid. HMO insurance is usually less expensive because the insured pays flat fees and accepts the HMO's doctors and procedures.

The deductible amount should be low enough for you to absorb in any one year, but high enough to create a premium reduction. A family annual deductible is a logical arrangement because more people are absorbing the risk.

Most insurers have participation clauses which require you to pay 20% to 25% of the covered charges in excess of the deductible. Look for participation limits in your contracts so that you do not participate in the expenses beyond a certain maximum. For example, if you have a policy which has a $500 deductible with a $10,000, participation limitation, and $14,500 worth of medical expenses are incurred, your cost would be $3,000 (25% of $10,000 plus the $500 deductible). The insurance company's share would be $11,500. If you did not have the participation limitation, your cost would have been $4,000 (25% of $14,000, plus the $500 deductible).

Be sure that you have major medical coverage!

MEDICARE SUPPLEMENTAL INSURANCE AND LONG TERM HEALTH CARE
Medicare is a federal health insurance program for people 65 or older, people of any age with permanent kidney failure and certain disabled people. The best source for information on this program is your local Social Security Administration office but in the meantime the following should be helpful.

SOME THINGS YOU NEED TO KNOW ABOUT MEDICARE
Medicare has two parts: hospital insurance and medical insurance. Hospital insurance, which pays for in-patient hospital and certain follow-up care, is financed through the social security tax (FICA). Medical insurance, which helps pay for doctors' and many other medical services, is financed by general federal revenues and by the monthly premiums paid by people who have enrolled in it.

The medical care part of Medicare insurance (called part B) pays for 80% of the "reasonable and customary" charges after a $75 per year deductible. All too often there is a serious discrepancy between what Medicare considers reasonable and what you are charged. For example, let's say that you have a kidney operation and the charges look like this:

1.	Doctor's charge for operation	$50,000
2.	Medicare's definition of reasonable	$30,000
3.	Medicare pays 80% of #2	$24,000
4.	YOU PAY (#1 minus #3)	$26,000

In this case medicare pays only 48% of the total charge and you pay the difference! To protect yourself, you need to buy Medicare supplemental insurance. This is purchased after you turn 65. Coverage and cost vary; so you should shop.

At first it would appear that the hospitalization part of Medicare (part A) would be adequate; after the patient pays $520, Medicare pays 100% of the hospital costs for the first 60 days, all but $130 per day for days 61 through 90, and all but $260 per day for days 91 through 150. However there is a problem. Medicare pays hospitals according to "diagnosed" illness. Each illness has a predetermined hospital charge which the government is willing to pay to the hospital regardless of how long a patient uses the facility. So, for example, if the predetermined cost of a kidney operation is $30,000 and the hospital can get a patient out at a cost of $15,000, more profit can be made. The final result is that patients are forced to leave the hospital before they should, only to find they must have supplemental nursing care.

Medicare will not pay for custodial nursing home care and these costs can be very high. According to the American Health Care Association, half of all people over the age of 65 will require nursing home care. When you approach 65, you should buy long term health care insurance unless you have unlimited assets. Though congress is strengthening Medicare coverage, prolonged illnesses can be a financial catastrophe. Make sure the policy you buy covers custodial care and, as with any insurance, shop before you buy.

AUTOMOBILE INSURANCE

If you own an automobile, you need auto insurance. In many states it is a crime to drive without it.

THINGS YOU NEED TO KNOW ABOUT AUTOMOBILE INSURANCE

There are seven types of coverage which all insurers offer. Some you need; some you don't. You do, however, need to understand them before you make the decisions.

1. **Bodily Injury Liability.** If you cause an accident which kills or hurts another person, this part of your auto insurance covers any legal costs and any legal liability. You must have this coverage. If you live in a no-fault state, you will need less liability coverage because each insurance company pays for an accident no matter whose fault it is. The laws were created to avoid lawsuits. Nevertheless, you should still carry a minimum of $100,000 if you can afford it. If you have substantial assets carry at least $300,000, and supplement your policy with an umbrella policy (called umbrella because they "cover" your original policy by providing supplemental coverage cheaply). This will greatly increase your coverage for a small increase in your premium.

2. **Collision Coverage.** This insurance pays for the cost of repairing your own car. Because the odds you will damage your own car and therefore collect on this insurance are greater than the odds of collecting on the 6 other types of coverage, collision insurance is the largest part of your premium. The higher the deductible, the lower your cost. It is

important to remember the fact that insurance companies will pay only market or book value for your car; so the older it gets, the less will be paid to fix it. No matter how much insurance you own, an insurance company will never pay more than the market or book value. As your car approaches extinction, you may want to stop or reduce this coverage.

3. **Comprehensive Coverage.** This includes theft, glass breakage, damage from vandalism or fire, flood or other acts of God. It is coverage you should have.

4. **Medical Payments Coverage.** This pays for doctor and related hospital bills that come about as the result of an accident. You and your passengers are covered.

5. **Property Damage Liability.** This portion of the policy pays for property damage caused by you while driving your car. If, for example, you ran into somebody's house, you would be protected. You should carry at least $50,000 of it.

6. **Uninsured Motorists Coverage.** Even though it is against the law in most states to drive without insurance, some people do it anyway. This insurance will protect you and your passengers if the other driver is not insured or if you are the victim of a hit-and-run accident. It covers medical expense, loss of wages, pain and suffering. You should have this protection.

7. **Underinsured Motorists Coverage.** If you are in an accident which was somebody else's fault, and that person was underinsured, this part of the policy would cover the difference for liability claims. This coverage is not mandatory, but quite desirable and not very expensive.

Some cars may be uninsurable or very expensive to insure. Insurance companies know which are the cars that have problems such as a high vulnerability to theft or mechanical weaknesses. You should check out the insurability of a car before you buy it.

Premium discounts are available for factors such as a good driving record, multicar coverage, a mature driver, the installation of anti-theft devices, driver training and defensive driving courses taken, restricted mileage usage, non-smoker, good student, rural location, a safe car, and passive seat belts or air bags. These discounts can add up to substantial savings; so be sure to ask your agent about them.

Although your driving record will help determine your premiums, it is your car that is insured. So if somebody else is driving your car with your permission, your insurance will cover everything it would have covered if you were driving.

Riders are expensive and you probably do not need them. For example, often salespeople will try to sell you accidental death insurance as a rider. If you already have life insurance, you do not need this.

Shop before you buy. I suggest you use a matrix similar to that shown below. Periodically, the Los Angeles Times publishes comparative auto insurance information. Other newspapers may also.

		PREMIUM		
COVERAGE TYPE	AMOUNT	COMPANY A	COMPANY B	COMPANY C
Bodily Liability	$100-300,000	_____	_____	_____
Collision ($250 ded.	car value	_____	_____	_____
Comprehensive	$25,000	_____	_____	_____
Medical Payments	$5,000	_____	_____	_____
Property Damage	$50,000	_____	_____	_____
Uninsured Motorist	$30,000	_____	_____	_____
Underinsured Motorist	$30,000	_____	_____	_____

HOMEOWNERS INSURANCE

Whether you own a home or not, you should understand homeowners insurance. It involves much more than fire insurance and will cover at least the following:

1. Damage to your home or appended structure.

2. Liability for which you are found responsible no matter where you are in the world (with a few exceptions).

3. Damage and theft to any of your property, with certain exceptions such as your car.

4. Living expenses while your house is being repaired because of fire or other covered catastrophe.

5. Injury to someone else on your property.

Here are some things to remember when you are buying homeowners insurance:

For a long time, insurance companies encouraged people to buy 80% coverage. One hundred percent coverage was expensive and considered superfluous since very rarely was a home destroyed 100%. However, the public became disenchanted with this kind of coverage when inflation in the 1970's and early 1980's created a situation wherein homes continually were underinsured. Additionally, the formulas which the insurance companies used for paying claims were confusing and unintelligible to most consumers, resulting in law suits and unhappy customers. Responding to this, insurers now offer insurance policies that are guaranteed to pay replacement cost. This type of insurance solves the problem of changing values and labor costs. Instead of determining the SALES VALUE of the house at the time the insurance is purchased, the insurance companies determine the REPLACEMENT COST.

There are various types of policies available with titles H01, HO2, HO3, HO4, HO5, HO6, and HO8. Each of these is a different quality. HO3 is the one that most homeowners need and buy. It is the best value. HO5 is the most comprehensive and is also the most expensive. If you are a renter or an owner of a cooperative, you can cover the contents of your domicile and buy liability insurance at the same time by purchasing an HO4 policy.

Certain contents of your house such as jewelry are usually not covered by your homeowners insurance. However, you can buy a "floater" which will cover them. The floater covers a category of items and the total dollar value covered is usually limited to $10,000. An "endorsement," on the other hand, covers a specific item. For example, if you have an expensive ring, you should purchase an endorsement to protect it because a floater probably won't be enough.

Since insurers will pay only for the value of your possessions or home, it is important to make sure you outline these values. In the case of your home, the best thing you can do is have it appraised for insurance purposes. As for the contents, make sure you have an inventory of what you own and what each item is worth. Keep this inventory in some other location. Video tapes or pictures will help establish that you did, in fact, possess the contents you are claiming were lost or destroyed.

Check to see whether your insurer offers discounts for such things as smoke alarms, senior citizens, burglar alarms, non-smokers, and sprinkler systems.

No matter how much money you spend on insurance, you are spending it for something you hope will not pay off. In the next few chapters we will talk about spending money in ways which you DO hope will pay off.

CHAPTER 8

DEVELOPING PERSPECTIVE

Your frame of reference, particularly if you very recently became "alone with your money" because of death or divorce, has been affected by the emotional trauma you have been experiencing. Gone is the structure that provided a basis for your life, in particular for your security.

In the first chapters of this book you started to create a new structure designed to help you get the money part of your life together. If you completed all the exercises you should now have down on paper a realistic view of your financial situation and can look at the facts and figures, whatever emotional turmoil you are experiencing. I hope you have shed your old attitudes about money, and rid yourself of old judges, such as your parents or prior mate. You have determined your money needs, and you have set financial goals. Now that you have a rational perspective of your personal financial reality, you are better prepared to make informed investment decisions.

Still, the process is understandably frightening. The decisions you make are important and may be critical. Success or failure could have a great impact on the rest of your life. The choices seem to be infinite. They are complicated and specialized, requiring technical and economic knowledge and understanding. You may not be interested or comfortable with these subjects. Investing is a dynamic process, always changing and always affected by macro events such as war, emerging technologies, government policies, new tax laws and changes in world trade. Investors have no way to control these events and experts have different interpretations. So how is it possible for an ordinary person to make intelligent decisions without taking risks? The answer is that it isn't. But it is possible to develop a perspective which will make the risks tolerable. It is possible to eliminate choices which are not consistent with your situation or comfort zone.

People who are experienced investors, or who do a lot of research before making up their minds, invest with an enviable peace of mind. Their perception of the risks associated with the investments they are considering is close to the reality of those risks. They have developed a structure which guides their decision making.

It is much easier to make investment decisions when you have the benefit of experience and education. Logically, it would follow that when you are ready to invest, if you want to do it with a high degree of comfort, you should learn everything you possibly can about the universe of investment choices and about the particular investments you are considering.

But logic is not always the predominant force in making decisions or taking action, particularly when one has recently been thrown off balance by a death or divorce. Most people do not have the time or inclination to take on the research that is necessary to make fully-informed investment decisions. Work, family, or other activities are more important to them. So the challenge is to develop a realistic investment perspective of risk and rewards, one which will facilitate making decisions with a high degree of comfort, even when you do not have the wherewithal to consider the universe of options.

The next few chapters will help you build your investment perspective and will make it easier for you to make specific investment decisions.

CHAPTER 9

WHAT REWARDS SHOULD YOU EXPECT FROM INVESTING?

If someone offered you an investment in which the principal was absolutely guaranteed, which paid 13% interest (when government bonds are paying 9%), promised to grow 14% per year, and had tax advantages to offset all the interest, would you want to buy it? Of course you would. If you did buy it, you probably would lose your money. The old investment saying "If it looks too good to be true, it probably is," is valid. But it is human nature to want it all.

Webster defines "sucker" as "a person easily fooled or cheated; a person readily drawn to specified attractions." When it comes to investing "There is a sucker born every day." This is not because people are stupid, but because they make decisions inspired by unrealistic expectations.   When unrealistic expectations are combined with greed, it is easy to get "sucked" into a bad investment. To avoid this you need to remember the following:

- THERE IS ONLY SO MUCH JUICE IN AN ORANGE!

- THE RETURN ON ANY INVESTMENT IS RELATIVE TO ITS RISK

THERE IS ONLY SO MUCH JUICE IN AN ORANGE!

If you go to the refrigerator, take out an orange and squeeze it as hard as you can, you are going to get only so much juice out of it. This is true with investments too. There is only so much you can get out of an investment! Therefore there is only so much you should expect.

There are four rewards available to you when you invest:

Safety of Principal
Safety of Buying Power (Growth)
Income
Tax Advantages

SAFETY OF PRINCIPAL means that the dollars you invest will be safe and will be returned to you.

SAFETY OF BUYING POWER means that when the dollars are returned, they will be worth at least what they were when you invested them. If you invest $10,000 today and inflation is 5%, in order for it to be worth the same $10,000 in 10 years, you will have to get back $16,289. Another word for safety of buying power is "growth." The money must grow to compensate for inflation. To get safety of principal you might want to put your money in a bank, whereas to get safety of buying power, you might want to invest in the stock market or real estate.

INCOME means that the investment will produce income. For example, if you lend your money to some institution such as a bank, it will pay you interest income while using your money.

TAX ADVANTAGE means that the investment will provide "write-offs" that will allow you to reduce the amount of taxes you are paying. Prior to the tax act of 1986 there were many investments which allowed you to use losses (often just on paper) as write-offs against other income. This was an immediate benefit to people, and tax shelters were quite popular. Congress eliminated most of the tax write-offs it had previously created when passing the 1986 law; so tax advantages are not as available as they used to be. However, one of the things that Congress seems to be consistent about is changing tax laws. As our government wants to encourage investing in certain kinds of industries, tax advantages will once again be allowed.

Let's take a look at a couple of investment oranges and see why there is only so much juice in them.

From the standpoint of safety of principal, the safest investment is a United States government obligation such as a Treasury Bill (T. Bill). It is safe because the full faith and credit of the United States Government is behind it and if the government has to, it can print money to pay you back. T. Bills pay interest but it is about the lowest interest available. Why? Because it is the safest investment. There are no tax advantages, and there is no safety of buying power. So unless there is no inflation, the juice of this investment is made up mostly of safety of principal.

Let's compare this to a real estate investment. There are two ways to buy real estate: with all cash, or through the use of a mortgage, i.e. borrowed money. If you buy an apartment house and you pay cash for it, you have relative safety of principal because even if all the tenants leave, you do not have to worry about foreclosure since you have not borrowed any money which must be repaid. Income from a real estate investment is equal to rents less expenses. Since no mortgage or interest payment is owed, the net income should be fairly high, assuming the apartment house is filled and the expenses of maintaining and managing are reasonable. The value of the property will grow as rents go up; therefore there is potential safety of buying power which will be realized when the property is sold.

Let's assume that instead of paying all cash for the apartment, you pay 20% down and borrow 80%. Now you will get a different mixture of juice out of this investment. There is now less safety of principal because there is some danger you will not be able to pay the mortgage. If, for some reason, revenue from rents dropped, there might not be enough money to make the monthly payment. This could result in foreclosure and you could lose your principal. Additionally, there is less income because the mortgage interest and principle must be paid every month.

You are giving up income and safety of principle; what juice is being added? Now, because there is a mortgage, there are more tax advantages. The interest paid on the mortgage is deductible.

The biggest change, however, is in the potential return on the dollars invested (growth) that the investment now offers. To understand this, it is necessary to look at some numbers and to compare buying the same apartment house without a mortgage and with a mortgage. Let's pretend that you have $500,000 cash and you buy an apartment house for $500,000, paying all cash for it. Let's also assume that your apartment house will grow in value 5% per year for the next 5 years. At the end of five years your building will be worth $638,000. If you sell it, your total profit (excluding tax considerations and cash flow) will be $138,000. This means that over a period of five years, your $500,000 investment will earn 27.6%. To calculate this divide the $138,000 profit by the $500,000 investment.

Now let's pretend that instead of putting all your $500,000 into the apartment house, you put $100,000 down and borrowed $400,000. Your total profit is still $138,000 but instead of earning 27.6% on your investment, you have earned 138% because you personally invested only $100,000 not $500,000. (To calculate this, divide your profit of $138,000 by $100,000, your cash invested). This amounts to about 3.5 times more return on your investment than if you paid for it with all cash. This example is exaggerated because it does not include the higher cash flow obtainable in an all cash investment. However, it does illustrate the point and is an excellent example of the "There is only so much juice"in an orange" concept. If you own the apartment free and clear you will have safety of principal and income. If you are willing to give up the safety of principal and the income, you will get tax advantages and greater growth potential.

During the tax shelter days, it was easy to forget that there is only so much you can get out of any one investment. People were willing to invest in tax shelters because they knew they were going to lose money by sending it to the government (forgetting social considerations). Either because they had not set aside enough money or because they just didn't want to pay taxes, people purchased investments that they would not have bought otherwise. The thinking was "Oh, well, what do I have to lose? Much of the cost of this investment is being paid for with money I would have had to pay in taxes. If I get anything back, I will be ahead." The trouble is that most people forgot or did not realize the "only so much juice in an orange" concept. They bought tax shelters, got their tax advantages (although sometimes these were disallowed by the IRS), and then over time forgot that they could not expect safety of principal, income, and growth too! Sometimes they lost it all.

You too will lose if you forget that there is only so much available from any one investment. Greed interferes with common sense. Although there are many examples of investors' being taken advantage of because of bad people, you must take responsibility for making the decision to invest. By understanding that there is only so much one investment can produce you have taken a big step toward developing a perspective for making good investment decisions. The next question is, "How much should you expect to earn on an investment?"

THE RETURN ON ANY INVESTMENT IS RELATIVE TO ITS RISK

All potential returns on investments are related to the risks inherent in those investments. Why is that so? People who want to raise money, either through loans or equity (ownership), want to pay as little as possible to do this. The first concern investors have is that they want to get their money back. So if someone who wants to raise money can guarantee the money will be returned, he will need to pay less for the use of that money. The safer the investment is, the less borrowers have to pay.

Historically the financial market has earned a 3% to 3.5% "real" return on its money. "Real" return means total interest paid (sometimes called "nominal" interest) less inflation. So if the nominal or total interest rate paid on an investment is 8.5%, it means that people who are lending money think the annual inflation rate

125

will average 5 to 5.5% during the period for which they are lending the money.

Your perspective on what to expect from an investment should start with a United States Government obligation. Today, as this book is being written, 90 day T. Bills are paying 6.8% interest and 30 year T. Bonds are paying 9.7%. Why is there a difference? Each has an equal amount of safety. Additionally, the real rate of return on both will be 3% to 3.5%. The difference in the nominal rate of return is a reflection of how the financial community perceives inflation over a period of time. In the case of the T. Bond, lenders and borrowers are guessing that during a thirty year period inflation will average approximately 6.2% (9.7% nominal rate minus a 3.5% real interest rate), whereas they are assuming that for the next 90 days inflation will be at the rate of 3.3% (6.8 % nominal rate minus 3.5% real rate).

The value in knowing these facts is that they give you a point of reference or "benchmark." You can compare the investment you are looking at with T. Bills or T. Bonds. If you are considering an investment which is paying 14% interest when T. Bills are paying 6.8% your first question should be "Why?" The fact that an investment is claiming to pay so much more than the safest investment available does not mean there is anything wrong with the investment. It just means that there is more risk, and you need to find out what the additional risks are before you invest. This can be done through your own research, checking with your financial planner, or talking to your broker. Your local library may employ a business librarian who could be a source of information also.

The results of a study conducted by Ibbotson Associates of Chicago comparing the cumulative compounded return of various kinds of investments over a 60 year period are quite useful in developing a perspective on what to expect as a return on your investment. Here are the 1927-1987 results:

INVESTMENT TYPE	CUMULATIVE COMPOUNDED RETURN
All Stocks	9.8%
Small Stocks	12.6%
Long Term Corporate Bonds	4.8%
Long Term Government Bonds	4.1%
U.S. Treasury Bills	3.4%

As this part of the book is being written, we have apparently just completed a bull market, the longest in the history of the stock market. Annual returns of 25% to 30% have been common for stocks and mutual funds. The Ibbotson figures show that during the 60 year period studied, the cumulative compounded return was 9.8%. This should tell you that 25% to 30% is high and probably will not continue forever. A 9.8% return is more likely. Nobody likes to see the value of his or her investment shrink, but having an historical perspective can keep you from going crazy when it happens.

Understanding the magic of compounding is the last link you need in developing a perspective of what to expect. Over a period of time, the difference between 4.1% and 9.8% is enormous when those returns are being compounded. In Appendix C is a matrix which shows the cumulative compounded value of $1,000 over different periods of time and assuming different rates of return. To calculate how much a particular investment would grow, find the number of years you will be investing and, moving across the page, stop in the column under the rate you expect to earn. Then multiply that number times the number of $1,000's you are investing. For example, a $10,000 investment in a government bond growing at the compounded rate of 4.1% will be worth $33,380 in 30 years (multiply 10 times 3,338). However a $10,000 investment in common stocks earning 9.8% would be worth $165,220 in the same time period. That is a difference of $131,840, or 400% more! You might ask, "Why bother with government bonds?" The answer has to do with PEACE OF MIND and the other side of rewards: RISK.

CHAPTER 10

HOW TO MANAGE THE RISKS OF INVESTING

An oxymoron is a figure of speech in which contradictory ideas or terms are combined, such as "jumbo shrimp" or "bureaucratic efficiency." A riskless investment is another oxymoron. No matter what you invest in, there is risk. No matter how hard you try, you cannot avoid it. But unlike some of the other risks you may be avoiding right now (such as new relationships), investment risks can be identified, sometimes they can be quantified, and they CAN be managed.

Because of this, investing can be quite useful, not only for financial reasons, but because accomplishment of the process can serve as a catalyst to build momentum for facing other aspects of your life.

There are four major risks of investing:

- INAPPROPRIATE CHOICE RISKS

- MARKET RISKS

- INFLATION/DEFLATION RISKS

- PEOPLE RISKS

These risks are on the other side of the "reward" coin and are the major reasons you can lose money while investing. By understanding them, you should be able to manage them.

MANAGING INAPPROPRIATE CHOICE RISKS

An inappropriate choice risk occurs when you buy an investment for the wrong reason. For example, you might buy an income oriented investment when you need growth. Or, when government T. Bonds are paying 9%, you might believe that you can get 20% from another type of investment without taking substantial risks. These sorts of risks are controlled by having a realistic perspective on what to expect from investments, knowing the reality of your financial situation, and what you need. These topics were discussed in previous chapters, and although rationally you know these things, fear and greed can interfere with your judgement. Fear often comes disguised as prudence, or rationality. Greed is actually another manifestation of fear--fear of being stupid and not getting as much as you think you should or fear of never having enough.

Many investment mistakes are caused by one or both of those emotions. The way to manage them is to ask yourself the following questions whenever you make an investment decision:

1. If I make this investment, what is the best thing that can happen?

2. If I make this investment, what is the worst thing that can happen?

3. If I make this investment, what is the most likely thing that will happen?

Unless you are fairly certain about number 3, you need to do some more thinking before you make your decision. Very rarely will either the best or the worst thing happen. You need to be able to live with the worst; you need to understand that the best is not to be expected; and you must have a very clear picture of the most likely result, as you will probably be living with that one.

MANAGING MARKET RISKS

On October 19, 1987, the Dow Jones Index fell approximately 500 points; it was the biggest single drop in the history of Wall Street. The crash of 1987 is a vivid reminder of the most important economic lesson you need to learn.

THE MARKET GOES UP AND IT GOES DOWN. It doesn't seem to matter whether it is the stock market, bond market, real estate, or oil. There is always market volatility. This volatility is caused by the forces of supply and demand. The reason the market crashed was that there were more sellers than there were buyers. Eventually, this turns around and prices start going back up.

Although market volatility is a major risk, it is also a friend. Without volatility it would be difficult to make money investing. If everybody knew when the market was going to go up and when it was going to go down, price differences would rarely occur. It is the differences that create the profit opportunities. Bernard Baruch once said, "The time to buy straw hats is in the winter."

This simple "buy low and sell high" philosophy is very clear to most investors. The central problem, of course, is knowing when the market is low and when is it high. When should you buy and when should you sell? Timing is what makes investing so difficult. Reasonable people reach different conclusions with the same data. Sometimes they win and sometimes they lose. Sometimes you will win and sometimes you will lose.

Macro-economic dynamics such as war, change in government policy, foreign political upheavals or natural disasters will affect investor psychology, which in turn will influence supply and demand. These are things that can neither be anticipated with accuracy nor controlled by individual investors, even the most sophisticated and experienced professionals. How can inexperienced neophytes expect to win with this kind of uncertainty? Can you who are alone with your money for the first time manage this enormous market risk? The answer is yes! The techniques are so simple, I feel like the proverbial doctor whose universal cure for most maladies is to take an aspirin and go to bed. Nevertheless, if you follow these tried but true guidelines, your chances for success are significant improved.

1.   KEEP AN ADEQUATE CASH OR CASH EQUIVALENT RESERVE. The rule of thumb in the financial planning industry is 3 to 6 months' expenses. The amount you chose is a function of your level of comfort and certainty of your income. By having enough reserve, you will not have to sell your investments in a crisis situation at reduced prices.

2   DIVERSIFY your investments. This means, for example, that if you are going to invest in the stock market, do not buy just one stock, buy many. Additionally, instead of putting all your money into one KIND of investment, such as stocks or real estate, spread it around. Often, when one kind of investment is doing well, another is doing poorly and your investment portfolio tends to balance itself out.

When you do not have enough money to create diversification yourself (which is usually the case), the following investment vehicles are useful:

   a.   MUTUAL FUNDS. When you purchase a mutual fund, you are buying an investment which has as its underlying asset a diversified portfolio. So instead of having $10,000 invested in one or two stocks, you can invest in a mutual fund and get 25 to 300 different stocks.

   b.   LIMITED PARTNERSHIPS or TRUSTS for real estate, oil and other investments. Although these methods of investing have received some bad press, it was not the investment structure that didn't work; it was either the management or the underlying economics of the particular investments. So you should remain open to these investment vehicles. They can offer excellent opportunities for diversification. For as little as $5,000 it is possible to buy a small portion of many different pieces of real estate, oil wells or whatever underlying properties the partnership is buying.

3. BE A LONG TERM, not a short term, investor. Ibbotson's study drives this point home by comparing investment results with four different holding periods over a 60 year time frame.

The study showed the following results for common stocks:

a. In the 60 one year periods studied, there were 19 periods of negative returns. The highest one year return was a plus 53.9% and the lowest was minus 43.3%.

b. In the 56 five year periods studied, there were seven periods of negative returns. The highest five year return was a plus 23.8% and the lowest was minus 12.5%.

c. In the 51 ten year periods studied, there were only two periods with negative returns. The highest ten year return was a plus 20.1% and the lowest was a minus .9%.

d. In the 36 twenty-five year periods studied, there were no negative returns. The highest twenty-five year return was a plus 14.7% and the lowest was a plus 5.9%.

These figures show that as the time period increases, both the highs and the lows decrease.

Although it is possible to make money investing in shorter time periods, the odds that you will lose money are increased. If you are considering investing in the stock or bond market, do not do it unless you are willing to commit your money for at least 5 years. When investing in real estate be willing to commit to at least 10 years.

MANAGING INFLATION/DEFLATION RISK

After reading about market risk, you might be asking yourself "Why invest at all?" Perhaps you want to build your net worth for security, for financial freedom, or for the ability to acquire things. But if none of those things is important to you, protecting your assets against inflation should be.

Because inflation erodes the value of cash, it is necessary to buy investments which will grow at least as much as inflation. As inflation increases, our economy tends to weaken and often we go into a recession or a depression. When this happens, cash is a good asset to hold. Tangible assets, such as real estate, traditionally do well during inflationary periods. However, having too much of your portfolio in real estate can be dangerous because real estate is illiquid and difficult to sell when prices are going down.

So, on the one hand it is necessary to protect your assets from inflation, and on the other, you should guard against the possibility of deflation. Diversification is one answer to this dilemma. Another is flexibility.

The way to have flexibility is to make sure enough of your portfolio is liquid (can easily be cashed out). At the time of this writing, because we are in a particularly unstable period, I am suggesting that my clients keep at least 70% of their investment assets (not including a home) in liquid form. I consider an asset liquid that can be cashed in within two weeks. This much liquidity provides the ability to make changes quickly. The big question is, "When will you KNOW that it is time to change the balance of liquidity?"

The answer is that you never will KNOW for sure. The best you can do is to make an educated guess. Most likely you will depend on help from other people to make your decisions. And that brings us to the next type of risk.

MANAGING PEOPLE RISKS

There are two kinds of investing, active and passive. Each has its advantages, disadvantages, risks and rewards. However, in each case, in one way or another you will use other people to help. For example, if you want to invest in an apartment house as an active investor, you can go out and purchase it, rent it, manage it, and ultimately sell it. You might require the services of a broker to buy and sell it, and a manager to manage it. An alternative would be to invest as a passive investor in a limited partnership in which the general partner buys the apartment, rents it, manages it, and sells it. In either case, other people are involved.

Most people decide to be passive investors. They recognize they do not have the time, energy, inclination, or ability to be successful active investors. So what passive investors need is people who do have the time, energy, inclination and ability to make the kind of judgements they themselves are not willing to make. Passive investors also need to work with people who are honest.

Judgment and honesty are the two most important people qualities needed to mitigate risk. Of the two, honesty is probably the more important because when business mistakes are made, and they will be, it is better to have a partner who acknowledges and addresses the problems rather than covering them up. Mistakes that are covered up simply create more problems.

How do you find both judgement and honesty when making a passive investment? You do something the investment community calls "due diligence." Due diligence is another word for research, or checking into the background of the people sponsoring an investment, as well as investigating the investment itself. To understand this process, you need to understand how most investments are distributed to the public.

134

Let's say, for example, that a sponsor (somebody who wants to raise money to buy real estate--sometimes called a general partner or syndicator) needs to raise $5,000,000 and does not have friends with enough money to cover it all. His alternative is to try to attract other investors. He does this by creating a limited partnership in which limited partners put up the money for the project and he, as general partner, manages it. He can either try to find investors himself (in an unregulated mode so long as he is not getting more than 35 investors) or he can use the securities industry channels of distribution.

If he decides to offer his investment through the securities industry, he will first create an offering memorandum which describes the investment and discloses all relevant and known risks. He will then try to get broker dealers (such as Merrill Lynch, Dean Witter, or many other smaller firms) to approve the offering so that their sales forces can sell it. Broker dealers are regulated by the National Association of Stock Dealers, a self-regulating body which has very strict guidelines and regulations. The NASD requires all broker dealers to perform "reasonable due diligence" before agreeing to sell a product. This due diligence may consist of reading the offering memorandum, examining the books of the general partners, doing background searches, and visiting the actual sights of the properties being offered for sale. If the broker dealer approves it for sale, then the registered representatives (people who have passed certain examinations required by the NASD) can sell it, and these representatives are required to do their own due diligence also on the same product. They do not have to repeat everything their broker dealer did, but they must understand the investment before selling it. This entire procedure acts like a filtering system in which various people along the way are making value judgements about the investment itself and about the ability and integrity of the people sponsoring it.

When you are choosing an investment advisor or broker, you need to do your "due diligence." Here is what to look for:

1. Experience. Although being in a business for a long period of

time is no guarantee of competence, it does mean that he or she has experience to draw on. Many common mistakes will have been made before you arrived. Ask if they have been through a a down market. Look for a minimum of 5 years.

2. Education. Formal education is useful and important, and continuing education is even more so. Find out what your advisor does to keep his knowledge up-to-date. Look for somebody who does not rely on just one source of information, such as the Wall Street Journal.

3. Successes and Failures. Ask your potential advisor to tell you about both. What people learn from their successes or failures will influence future judgement. If your potential advisor cannot tell you about these lessons, move on. Everybody at one time or another makes mistakes or has failures. An unwillingness to talk about them can indicate immaturity, dishonesty or that he or she is not learning from experience.

4. Track Records. Although these can be important for judging how well somebody or some type of investment vehicle has done in the past, they can sometimes be deceptive. For example, a mutual fund with a fabulous 15 year history may no longer be using the portfolio manager who was responsible for creating that record. A real estate syndicator who shows a very high rate of return for previous investments may have created a successful track record with investments that are different from the one he is currently offering. Remember that people who are trying to sell you investments will do everything they can to show you the best track record possible. That's fine, but you should dig beneath the surface to find out whether the past performance is really relevant to the success of the investment you are currently considering.

5. Do not do business with anybody who is unwilling to disclose to you what you need to know in order to make your investment decisions. You are entitled to be told about all known risks before you invest. When you purchase an investment such as

a limited partnership, trust or mutual fund through a broker, he is required by law to give you an offering memorandum or prospectus. These will disclose known risks. If you purchase a stock, you are entitled to see statements disclosing the financial condition of the company.

6. Do not do business with people who have been convicted of violating securities laws or have a criminal record of any type. People do change, and criminals should be given a second chance, but there is no reason to give them a chance with your money.

7. Unless you are absolutely confident about the background of somebody who asks you to invest in something, deal only with licensed NASD brokers. Although there is no guarantee that these people will be honest, there is some legal recourse if they are not.

8. Checking out references can be a mixed bag, depending on how you get the references. Because the person you are checking is going to give you the most favorable reference possible, you will not get objectivity. If you have been referred to an advisor by a friend or another advisor, you probably have a better chance.

When choosing advisors, remember the words of Harry Truman "The buck stops here." You are the one who is ultimately responsible for taking care of YOUR money. Once you have chosen your advisors, you need to pay attention to what is going on. Only by doing this can you actively manage the risks that you will inevitably be taking.

Although there are other risks to think about when considering a specific investment, if you understand and manage the 4 major ones:

INAPPROPRIATE CHOICE RISKS

MARKET RISKS

INFLATION/DEFLATION RISKS

PEOPLE RISKS

you will have taken a major step in protecting your money and your future.

CHAPTER 11

GETTING HELP

Before you start looking for help, you should decide what kind of help you want.

Do you want someone to assist with your overall financial planning, including estate planning, tax planning, retirement planning, asset planning, and insurance planning? If so, I recommend that you use a Certified Financial Planner (CFP). The CFP designation identifies an individual who has completed the extensive educational, testing, and work experience requirements of the International Board of Standards and Practices for Certified Financial Planners (IBCFP) and has agreed to adhere to the IBCFP Code of Ethics by signing the IBCFP Declaration. Because anybody can call himself or herself a financial planner, the financial planning industry felt that it was necessary to identify those planners who have been formally educated in financial planning and who are willing to adhere to ethical standards set by the industry.

The IBCFP was formed for that purpose. Although the CFP designation does not guarantee competence or integrity it identifies those with the required education and a willingness to subscribe to ethical standards.

Do you want somebody to help with your overall financial planning and also with your investing? Use a CFP who is also a Registered Investment Advisor (RIA). If the planner is an RIA, ask to see his/her ADV form. An ADV is a disclosure form that RIA's are required by law to give to their clients. If you want to buy your investments from this same person, make sure that he or she is licensed with the National Association of Securities Dealers (NASD);

there must be an indication of this license displayed somewhere in the office.

Do you want somebody to give you investment advice only, without the other facets of financial planning? A CFP designation is helpful, but not mandatory. If you will be paying this person a fee for advice, he or she must be an RIA. If the person is simply selling you investments and is being compensated by commissions only, an RIA is not required but the NASD license is.

If you just want to buy some insurance, any licensed insurance salesperson can help you. But if you want additional expertise, use either a CFP or an insurance salesperson who is a Certified Life Underwriter (CLU). A CLU has passed examinations which require a more complete knowledge of insurance than is required simply to sell it.

Do you want some estate planning help? Although insurance salespeople with the CLU designation, CFP's and CPA's can identify your estate planning needs and make suggestions, ultimately you should use an attorney who specializes in estate planning. There is no designation for these specialists, but those who do concentrate on estate planning will let you know.

If you just want somebody to help you with your taxes, use a Certified Public Accountant (CPA). Once again, the CPA designation will not guarantee competence or integrity but in order for accountants to keep this designation, they must continue their education by attending at least 80 hours of classes every two years.

Whatever you decide, review the people risk considerations discussed in the previous chapter before you make a final decision. And I may as well confess that I have a bias toward the use of Certified Financial Planners in most of the types of circumstances discussed in this book. For that reason, the following section goes to some length to help you select the right one. Some of the criteria appy to other professionals as well.

HOW TO CHOOSE A CERTIFIED FINANCIAL PLANNER

If a friend or another professional recommends a particular CFP, by all means follow up on the lead. However, do not automatically use that person just because he or she is recommended by somebody you like or respect. If you rely totally on what someone else says, you may be disappointed. Your friends may have needs different from yours.

If an advisor that you are now using refers somebody, be sure to keep your objectivity. Professionals often get their business from other professionals' referrals. There is some potential danger in the "good old boy" system. This is not necessarily bad; it just means that you need to make your own decision based on what YOU think, not on what your referral source thinks. You need to find somebody with whom you are comfortable.

Often comfort is a function of "chemistry." To determine whether the chemistry is right, ask yourself the following questions:

1. Would I be willing to ask this person a question no matter how "stupid" it sounds? If the answer is "No," do not work with that planner. It is your money that is at stake, and you need to be encouraged to ask any questions you want. You literally cannot afford to be intimidated.

2   Do you like this person? If not, the relationship probably will not last very long.

But comfort or "chemistry" is not enough. You must also require integrity and ability. Asking the following questions will help you determine whether the person you are talking to has these qualities:

1. "Are you a member of either the Institute of Certified Financial Planners or the Registry of Financial Planners?"

The Institute of Certified Financial Planners is a non-profit professional organization of CFPs whose goals are to establish and maintain professionalism in financial planning, to promote the continued advancement of knowledge in the financial planning field, and to support programs increasing the abilities of CFP's to better service their clients. To maintain membership in the ICFP a CFP must have at least 30 units of continuing education per year.

The Registry of Financial Planners is a division of the International Association of Financial Planners (IAFP) which identifies those members who are practicing financial planners. The IAFP is a trade organization which has many members who are not financial planners. To be in the Registry the CFP must demonstrate that he or she actively writes financial plans. He or she must also pass an eight hour examination and is required to obtain at least 30 units of continuing education per year.

In addition to the continuing education requirements, members of both these organizations must adhere to a code of ethics which is designed to protect the public. Although no legal punitive action is taken by these organizations, they both are intent on purging those members who violate their codes of ethics. A few bad apples in a barrel can make the whole barrel seem rotten. The industry wants to protect the good ones, and this in turn helps to protect the public.

2. "Do you personally buy for yourself all the investments you recommend to clients?"

If the answer is "Yes," be careful. This is a two-edged sword. On the one hand, the planner thinks enough of the investments to buy them. On the other, he may be buying them simply to convince you to buy them. Different people have different financial planning needs. Planners are people too. They should have a wide variety of investments to sell, and it does not follow that they need every one themselves. If the answer is "Yes," ask "Why?" An honest answer would be "because I can't expect clients to buy something that I'm not willing to buy."

142

If the answer is "No," you probably won't have to ask why. The planner will explain it to you.

3.   "What do you think is going to happen to the economy?"

You want to know what the planner thinks will happen to interest rates, and why. What does he or she think the inflation/deflation outlook is, and why? What will general business conditions be, and why? The reason for asking these questions is not to believe or disbelieve the answers or to judge whether they are right or wrong. At any given time when you listen to economic experts, differing and various opinions may seem very plausible. Deciding who is right is difficult, to say the least.

What you really want to find out is whether thought has been given to the question and whether the answers are clear to you. Of course, if you have strong opinions of your own which seriously conflict with the answers you receive, you are probably better off not using that planner, unless the economic logic convinces you to change your mind.

4.   "What kind of return on my investments do you think you can get?"

It is important to notice how the planner answers this question. If you know that C.D.'S are running 7% and the planner tells you that you will probably earn 14%, you should shy away. This is far too aggressive. On the other hand, if C.D. rates are running around 10-11%, earning 13% or 14% could be reasonable.

Some good answers to this question are

a.   "I'm not sure what rate we will try to get. It depends on how aggressive we need to be in order to meet your goals."

b.   "I can't answer this question until I have allocated your assets to meet your goals."

c. "Much of this depends on your risk tolerance."

5. "How are you paid?"

If a planner is unwilling to tell you this, walk away. You have a right to know how, and you have a right to know how much. Planners are paid four different ways, with variations. Each method of payment has advantages and disadvantages to you.

    a. Commissions Only. The advantage is that you do not have to pay a fee for your plan. The disadvantage is the potential loss of objectivity because the planner must sell you something in order to get paid.

    b. Fee Only. The major advantage to this is that there is objectivity. Because the planner is getting paid to write the plan, there is no stake in having the client buy something. Although there are fee only plans that are very inexpensive, these are usually of the boiler plate computer-generated type. Personalized complex fee only plans are very expensive.

    c. Fee and Commissions. This is an attempt by planners to bring objectivity into the plan, keep the cost of the plan down and still make enough money. The advantages are that the plan fee will be less than fee only, and there will be more objectivity than if it were commissions only. The disadvantage is that the planner still needs to sell a product to you in order for him to make enough money. This could create some pressure on you to buy something.

    d. Fees reduced by commissions. With this method, the planner will quote realistic fees and use commissions paid to offset those fees. If, when the plan is implemented, there are no commissions to offset the fees, the total fees will be due. In most states, insurance commissions cannot be credited against fees. Additionally, the NASD limits the kinds of securities that the planner may use to offset commissions against fees. The advantage of this method to you is that you may end up paying little or no direct fee, and you still have the objectivity since the planner will be paid whether you buy or not. The disadvantage is that if you do not implement your plan, the fees will be higher than under the fee and commission method. This is because under the latter the planner quotes a lower fee assuming that commissions will make up the difference.

OTHER CONSIDERATIONS WHEN CHOOSING A PLANNER

APPEARANCE

A planner who dresses sloppily and has a messy office probably is someone to avoid. His appearance could be indicative of his work.

On the other hand, if he or she dresses expensively, has an expensive looking office and drives an expensive car, it does not necessarily mean that you have found a good planner. The person may simply enjoy expensive articles, but it could also mean that you are seeing a facade. The best con artists look the most successful. Why? Because they know that people are judged by how they look. It is human nature. Be careful of planners or other professionals who seem to flaunt their possessions. What you want is someone who can understand YOU and YOUR NEEDS.

IS IT BETTER TO DO BUSINESS WITH A PLANNER WHO DOES NOT IMPLEMENT?

Financial planning is about results, as well as planning. If you do business with a planner who tells you that you need to save $200,000 over a period of 10 years in order to fund your retirement but does not tell you specifically how to do it, you do not have a plan and you cannot implement it without further research. Much of implementation requires the purchase of investments or insurance. Planners who have products and create plans have the tools to help you implement your plan and accomplish your goals.

You want to be sure that the planner you use has a wide variety of investments from which he can chose to help you. If he or she uses only one company's products then your choices are limited.

NO LOAD VERSUS LOAD

No load is better if you want to do your own research and do not want service, ideas or advice, or if you are willing to pay a fee for these. Loads (commissions) are a way to pay for these services.

HOW MUCH SHOULD A PLAN COST?

Plans range in price from nothing (where the planner is being paid commission only) on up. The cost of the plan will depend on the type of plan that is being written and the complexity of the case.

For example, "boiler plate" plans are very inexpensive (from $100-$500). These are basically computer-generated plans in which suggestions are made generically based on parameters pre-established by computer programs. Often there is very little personal attention given and the plan is mailed to you.

Plans which are written specifically for you, with minimal boiler plate, and for which a planner spends time with you, will cost from $500 up. In California, the middle range of fees at this time is between $1500 and $3500. Some planners charge fees for writing plans that spell out what you need to do on a generic basis, and then charge "asset allocation" fees for making specific investment recommendations. You will find that there is no standard charge or method of charging.

Although it is important not to pay too much, it is more important that you get value.

YOUR IDEAL PLANNER RELATIONSHIP

If you were dependent entirely on your mate to make all the money decisions, you will need to be sure you don't try to establish your financial planner as a surrogate mate. The ideal relationship is one in which you make your own decisions and depend on your planner to give you the kind of information you need in order to do this intelligently.

YOUR IDEAL RELATIONSHIP WITH YOURSELF

This is a chance for you to restructure your life. By avoiding another dependency situation, you are becoming the dominant force in your life.

My goal in writing this book is to give people who are alone with their money enough self-confidence to make money decisions. If you have absorbed the contents of this book and have completed the various exercises, you know enough to start doing exactly that. You now have the tools to manage the financial part of your life. You know what you have, what you need, what you want, what risks to be aware of, what rewards to expect, and how to find and manage your helpers. You can do it. You now are actually better prepared than most people.

According to Judy Barber, a San Francisco money therapist, "The person who controls the money has the power." YOU NOW HAVE THE POWER. Yes, you are alone with your money, but you are also together with it. I hope that being together with your money will facilitate your being together with the rest of your life.

APPENDIX A

CAPITALIZATION   RATE

A capitalization rate (cap rate) is the expected rate of return on income-producing property in your area. For example, if a piece of real estate generates $15,000 per year in net operating income (all income minus all expenses except depreciation and debt service), and the local real estate and financial community estimates that 10% is a reasonable rate of return at this time for this kind of real estate, then to calculate the value of the property you divide the annual income ($15,000) by the cap rate (.10) to get a $150,000. This is the estimated value based on the cap rate.

Cap rates are subjective and depend upon how buyers view the specific piece of property and available alternative investments. To find out what the current cap rate in your area is, call your local real estate office or bank. It is possible that the person you talk with may not understand what you are asking because the concept is fairly sophisticated. Just ask whether there is anybody in the office who "thinks in terms of cap rates."

APPENDIX B

PLANNING FOR YOUR RETIREMENT

This is a repetitive process. You may as well go for everything you want in the first round and back off later.

1. First decide when you will retire. For planning purposes you need a goal; don't worry about the fact that you may not retire exactly at that time.

2. Then figure out how much you would need for living expenses on an annual basis if you were to retire today. Calculating this is easier than you think. Just use your CASH FLOW FORM and add or subtract the expenses that you would or would not have if you were retired. For example, if you plan to retire in 20 years and you know that your mortgage will be paid by that time, subtract your mortgage payment. If you weren't working now, would you travel more? How much more? You can quantify this by estimating your daily vacation expenses, and multiplying this figure by the number of days you think you would like to travel each year. When you have adjusted each detail line on your CASH FLOW FORM to reflect your retired life style, total all the figures.

3. Since you are not going to retire now, you must figure out how much this total annual amount will be when you do retire. This is calculated by multiplying today's estimate of retirement expenses by an inflation rate. So, for example, if you estimated that you need $50,000 a year for retirement today and you are not planning to retire for another 15 years, you will need approximately $83,700, assuming a 3.5% inflation rate.

If you have a financial calculator, enter a $50,000 PV (present value), a 3.5% I (interest) and a 15 N (number). Press the Future Value button; the number that comes up on the screen will be the

150

future value of the present estimated value of your annual retirement needs. Evaluate this for reasonableness before continuing.

For those of you who do not have a financial calculator, multiply the $50,000 by 1.035. This will give you the value of your $50,000 next year. Multiply this result by 1.035 to get the following year, and continue this compounding up to the year of your retirement. The number that you have calculated as of the date of your retirement will give you approximately the same living standard for one year as you calculated you would want today. However, it has been adjusted for inflation and is more realistic.

4. Next you need to determine how many dollars will be required for your total retirement period, from beginning to end. Deciding when you are going to die can be a problem. Actuarially, insurance companies generally use age 85. So if you retire at age 65 you will want to know how much it will cost to maintain the same standard of living for 20 years more. To do this, continue the compounding process starting at age 65 (or at whatever age you decide to retire), and add together each of these numbers until you have the total cost of your retirement. Using our example, the figures would look like this.

TOTAL COST OF RETIREMENT PERIOD

Year	Annual Amount Needed	Cumulative Amount Needed
1	$ 83,700	$ 83,700
2	$ 86,767	$ 170,466
3	$ 89,733	$ 260,199
4	$ 92,874	$ 353,073
5	$ 96,125	$ 449,198
6	$ 99,489	$ 548,687
7	$ 102,971	$ 651,658
8	$ 106,575	$ 758,233
9	$ 110,305	$ 868,538

Year	Annual Amount Needed	Cumulative Amount Needed
10	$ 114,166	$ 982,704
11	$ 118,162	$ 1,100,866
12	$ 122,297	$ 1,223,163
13	$ 126,578	$ 1,249,741
14	$ 131,008	$ 1,480,747
15	$ 135,593	$ 1,615,342
16	$ 140,339	$ 1,756,681
17	$ 145,251	$ 1,901,932
18	$ 150,330	$ 2,052,262
19	$ 155,597	$ 2,207,859
20	$ 161,043	$ 2,268,902

So statistically you will need $2,268,902 to pay for your 20 year retirement. If your family has a history of living longer, you should take that into account.

5. Now calculate the asset base which will be available at the time of retirement, given your present investments. First determine which of your assets will be available to finance your retirement. Figure out what percentage return they are earning (growth or income). Multiply this percentage by the reciprocal of your tax rate if the earnings are taxable. Using that result compound up to the year of retirement for each asset. Add all your assets together. This represents the total value of the assets which will be available to finance your retirement assuming you make no changes from now until then.

DO NOT INCLUDE YOUR HOUSE IN THIS LIST! The only exception is when you know you want to move. If that is the case, calculate your equity and subtract from your equity the total amount of money that would be required to pay for a substitute home if you were to move today. If you plan to rent rather than buy, add the rental to your expenses.

Now you have to make an assumption about how much income these assets will be able to produce when you retire. This should be expressed as a percentage and should be conservative. If you have used a 3.5% inflation rate in your expense calculation, then using a 4% after tax earnings rate would be conservative. Thus, $100,000 of retirement assets earning 4% after taxes would net $4,000 a year. Multiply the annual figure by the number of retirement years for a total of earnings for the period.

6. Next calculate income that will be coming to you from other sources, such as from pension plans and social security.

To estimate your social security benefits, contact your local social security office. If you have dealt with government agencies before, you know how frustrating it can be. Remember that they work for you, and that you are entitled to answers.

They may require that you send a formal request to Baltimore, or they may give you an answer directly. Either way, you should obtain a dollars and cents answer telling you how much your annual retirement benefits will be. Assuming that social security will still have COLA provisions (which increase your benefits by a cost of living allowance tied to inflation), compound your social security by an assumed COLA amount. I suggest that if you are using a 3.5% inflation rate, use the same COLA rate. Add all the annual benefits together to obtain a total for your retirement period.

Also find out whether any other non social security pension money you will be receiving will have COLA provisions. If so, follow the compounding process and add the results together. If not, just multiply the annual retirement benefit you will receive by the number of years of retirement.

7. Add your social security and non social security incomes and subtract from that your total expenses. This gives you your total net income during retirement. If it is negative, as it is in the example shown below, subtract the ASSETS AVAILABLE AT RETIREMENT. This is because it will be necessary to sell assets in order to pay for your retirement.

Total Earnings on Assets ($4,000 a year for 20 years) Available at Retirement	$80,000
Total other Income (Soc.Sec+Pension)	$700,000
Total Earnings and Income	$780,000
Total Expenses During Retirement (20years)	$2,268,092
Net Income During Retirement	($1,488,092)
ASSETS AVAILABLE AT RETIREMENT	$100,000
NET ASSETS AVAILABLE AFTER RETIREMENT	($1,388,092)

This tells you that your net income during retirement (expenses minus income) will be short by $1,488,092. After subtracting ASSETS AVAILABLE AT RETIREMENT the NET ASSETS AVAILABLE AFTER RETIREMENT in this sample are a minus $1,388,092. This is the additional amount of money you need to meet the retirement goal you set at the beginning. You can get it by saving, by creating a higher yield on your existing assets or by a combination of both.

However, to express this in today's dollars, you need to discount the $1,388,092 by the inflation rate you have been using. So if you have been using 3.5% then multiply the $1,388,092 by 96.5% for the last year; then that amount by 96.5% for every year until you have discounted to the present value. The discounted amount is $680,713. This represents the total additional amount of money you need in today's dollars.

Next this figure has to be translated into an annual savings rate. This is a complex calculation which requires a financial calculator. If you don't own one, I suggest you go to a stationery store and use theirs. If you do have one, the future value (FV) is the amount you are funding, which in our example is $683,713. "N" or number is the number of years that you have for funding. "I" is the interest assumption you make. Enter these three numbers and press "PMT" for payment. In our sample, I assumed an after tax earning of 6%, a 15 year period for funding and calculated that we would have to save approximately $29,000 a year to make up the shortage.

When the NET ASSETS AFTER RETIREMENT number is positive, it means that there will be money left in your estate when you die (assuming you die on schedule). If it is negative, then you need to accumulate at least that much money by doing one or more of the following:

   a.   Saving on an annual basis.

   b.   Repositioning your portfolio for a higher return (recognizing that the risk probably becomes higher also).

   c.   Combining "a" and "b."

This may require some adjustment in your lifestyle, but it is better to do it now, while there is time to accumulate, than to wait until it is too late.

APPENDIX C

COMPOUNDED RATE OF RETURN MATRIX

YEAR	4.10%	5.00%	5.30%	6.00%	6.50%	7.00%	8.00%	9.00%	9.80%	10.00%	11.00%
1	$1041	$1050	$1053	$1060	$1065	$1070	$1080	$1090	$1098	$1100	$1110
2	$1084	$1103	$1109	$1124	$1134	$1145	$1166	$1188	$1206	$1210	$1232
3	$1128	$1158	$1168	$1191	$1208	$1225	$1260	$1295	$1324	$1331	$1368
4	$1174	$1216	$1229	$1262	$1286	$1311	$1360	$1412	$1453	$1464	$1518
5	$1223	$1276	$1295	$1338	$1370	$1403	$1469	$1539	$1596	$1611	$1685
6	$1273	$1340	$1363	$1419	$1459	$1501	$1587	$1677	$1752	$1772	$1870
7	$1325	$1407	$1435	$1504	$1554	$1606	$1714	$1828	$1924	$1949	$2076
8	$1379	$1477	$1512	$1594	$1655	$1718	$1851	$1993	$2113	$2144	$2305
9	$1436	$1551	$1592	$1689	$1763	$1838	$1999	$2172	$2320	$2358	$2558
10	$1495	$1629	$1676	$1791	$1877	$1967	$2159	$2367	$2547	$2594	$2839
11	$1556	$1710	$1765	$1898	$1999	$2105	$2332	$2580	$2797	$2853	$3152
12	$1620	$1796	$1858	$2012	$2129	$2252	$2518	$2813	$3071	$3138	$3498
13	$1686	$1886	$1957	$2133	$2267	$2410	$2720	$3066	$3372	$3452	$3883
14	$1755	$1980	$2061	$2261	$2415	$2579	$2937	$3342	$3702	$3797	$4310
15	$1827	$2079	$2170	$2397	$2572	$2759	$3172	$3642	$4065	$4177	$4785
16	$1902	$2183	$2285	$2540	$2739	$2952	$3426	$3970	$4463	$4595	$5311
17	$1980	$2292	$2406	$2693	$2917	$3159	$3700	$4328	$4900	$5054	$5895
18	$2061	$2407	$2533	$2854	$3107	$3380	$3996	$4717	$5381	$5560	$6544
19	$2146	$2527	$2668	$3026	$3309	$3617	$4316	$5142	$5908	$6116	$7263
20	$2234	$2653	$2809	$3207	$3524	$3870	$4661	$5604	$6487	$6727	$8062
21	$2325	$2786	$2958	$3400	$3753	$4141	$5034	$6109	$7123	$7400	$8949
22	$2421	$2925	$3115	$3604	$3997	$4430	$5437	$6659	$7821	$8140	$9934
23	$2520	$3072	$3280	$3820	$4256	$4741	$5871	$7258	$8587	$8954	$11026
24	$2623	$3225	$3454	$4049	$4533	$5072	$6341	$7911	$9429	$9850	$12239
25	$2731	$3386	$3637	$4292	$4828	$5427	$6848	$8623	$10353	$10835	$13585
26	$2843	$3556	$3829	$4549	$5141	$5807	$7396	$9399	$11367	$11918	$15080
27	$2959	$3733	$4032	$4822	$5476	$6214	$7988	$10245	$12481	$13110	$16739
28	$3080	$3920	$4246	$5112	$5832	$6649	$8627	$11167	$13705	$14421	$18580
29	$3207	$4116	$4471	$5418	$6211	$7114	$9317	$12172	$15048	$15863	$20624
30	$3338	$4322	$4708	$5743	$6614	$7612	$10063	$13268	$16522	$17449	$22892

156

APPENDIX D

RECORD RETENTION

The normal statute of limitations (after which you cannot be held accountable or prosecutable on federal tax returns is three years. If you fail to file a return, or if there is a fraud, the statute of limitations never runs out. State statute of limitations will vary and sometimes are longer than federal. Listed below are some guidelines for retaining your records.

RECORDS	MINIMUM RETENTION PERIOD
Cancelled checks	3 years
Bank Deposit slips	3 years
Bank Statements	7 years (at least)
Tax returns	Permanent (you never know when you might need to refer to them.)
Home improvement receipts	Until you sell your house and complete your next tax return.
Expense records	3 years-If writing them off.
Entertainment records	3 years-if writing them off.
Limited partnership offerings	Until the investment is over.
Mutual fund statements	Until the investment is sold and taxes have been paid.
Brokerage statements	Same as mutual fund statements.
Insurance policies	Keep them until you are sure they are no longer in force.
Mortgages	Until paid or house is sold.
Contracts	Permanent
Minutes of corp. meetings	Life of company if your business.
Employee records	Period of employment of employee plus 3 years.
Depreciation records	Life of the business plus 3 years.
Journals and General Ledgers	Life of the business plus 3 years.
Inventory records	3 years.

APPENDIX E

NET WORTH FORM

DATE_____

ASSETS	AMOUNT
Checking Account	_____
Savings Accounts	_____
Money Market	_____
Certificate of Deposits	_____
Annuities	_____
Cash Value in Life Insurance	_____
Stocks	_____
Bonds	_____
Mutual Funds	_____
Municipal Bond Trusts	_____
Treasury Bills or Bonds	_____
Personal Residence	_____
Real Estate Other than Personal	_____
IRA's	_____
Vested Pension Plans	_____
Deferred Compensation	_____
Personal Business	_____
Personal Belongings	_____
Personal Loans	_____
Other Assets	_____
TOTAL ASSETS	_____

LIABILITIES	
Residence Mortgage	_____
Other Mortgages	_____
Credit Cards	_____
Bank Loans	_____
Margin Accounts	_____
Other Loans	_____
Other Debts	_____
TOTAL LIABILITIES	_____
NET WORTH (Assets minus Liabilities)	_____

APPENDIX F

CASH FLOW FORM

	LAST 12 MONTHS	ESTIMATE NEXT 12 MONTHS	COMMENTS

Date:_____

SOURCES OF TAXABLE
INCOME
Employment Income--His
Employment Income--Hers
Alimony
Pension--His
Pension--Hers
Social Security--His
Social Security--Hers
Dividends
Interest
Capital Gains
Taxable--Other
TOTAL TAXABLE INCOME

NON-TAXABLE INCOME
Child Support
Tax Free Municipal Bonds
Non Taxable--Other
TOTAL NON TAXABLE INCOME

TOTAL SOURCES OF INCOME

TAXES
Federal Income Taxes
State Income Taxes
FICA Taxes
Other
TOTAL TAXES

CASH FLOW CONT'D

	LAST 12 MONTHS	ESTIMATE NEXT 12 MONTHS	COMMENTS
NET INCOME AFTER TAXES	_____	_____	
COMMITTED EXPENSES			
HOUSING			
Mortgage Payment	_____	_____	
Rent	_____	_____	
Property Taxes	_____	_____	
Homeowners Insurance	_____	_____	
Utilities/Fuel	_____	_____	
Maintenance/Repair	_____	_____	
Other	_____	_____	
TOTAL HOUSING	_____	_____	
TRANSPORTATION			
Auto Loan Payments	_____	_____	
Insurance	_____	_____	
Gas/Oil/Repair	_____	_____	
Other (commuting, etc.)	_____	_____	
TOTAL TRANSPORTATION	_____	_____	
EDUCATION			
School and College	_____	_____	
Other	_____	_____	
TOTAL EDUCATION	_____	_____	
INSURANCE			
Life	_____	_____	
Disability	_____	_____	
Medical	_____	_____	
Other	_____	_____	
TOTAL INSURANCE	_____	_____	

CASH FLOW CONT'D

	LAST 12 MONTHS	ESTIMATE NEXT 12 MONTHS	COMMENTS
OTHER COMMITTED EXPENSES			
Food	_____	_____	
Clothing/Cleaning	_____	_____	
Phone	_____	_____	
Personal Care	_____	_____	
Medical Care	_____	_____	
Prescription Drugs	_____	_____	
Care for Dependents	_____	_____	
Repayment of Loans/Charges	_____	_____	
Business Meals & Travel	_____	_____	
Tax-Deductible--Other	_____	_____	
Non Tax-Deductible--Other	_____	_____	
Alimony	_____	_____	
TOTAL OTHER COMMITTED	_____	_____	
DISCRETIONARY EXPENSES			
Entertainment/Dining	_____	_____	
Vacation/Recreation/Club	_____	_____	
Gifts	_____	_____	
Hobbies	_____	_____	
Home Improvements	_____	_____	
Expenses for Long Term Goals	_____	_____	
Miscellaneous Purchases	_____	_____	
Tax-Deductible--Other	_____	_____	
Non Tax-Deductible--Other	_____	_____	
TOTAL DISCRETIONARY	_____	_____	
INVESTMENT OUTLAYS			
IRA	_____	_____	
Keogh	_____	_____	
Pension Plans	_____	_____	
Other Asset Purchases	_____	_____	

CASH FLOW CONT'D

	LAST 12 MONTHS	ESTIMATE NEXT 12 MONTHS	COMMENTS
TOTAL INVESTMENT OUTLAYS	_____	_____	
TOTAL EXPENSES	_____	_____	
NET CASH FLOW (negative)	_____	_____	

APPENDIX G

GOAL EVALUATION

GOAL	HOW MUCH	WHEN	IMPOR-TANCE	RANK
Retirement	_____	_____	_____	_____
Children's Education	_____	_____	_____	_____
More Spendable Income	_____	_____	_____	_____
Buy a New Car	_____	_____	_____	_____
Financial Security	_____	_____	_____	_____
Estate Plan	_____	_____	_____	_____
Insurance	_____	_____	_____	_____
Reduce My Taxes	_____	_____	_____	_____
Take Care of Sick Mother	_____	_____	_____	_____

APPENDIX H

GOALS RANKED

Rank	GOAL	HOW MUCH	WHEN
A	_____	_____	_____
B.	_____	_____	_____
C.	_____	_____	_____
D.	_____	_____	_____
E.	_____	_____	_____
F.	_____	_____	_____
G.	_____	_____	_____
H.	_____	_____	_____
I.	_____	_____	_____

APPENDIX I

BEFORE DIVORCE CASH FLOW

	CURRENT ANNUAL	CURRENT MONTHLY	% OF GROSS INCOME
SOURCES OF INCOME			
TAXABLE			
Employment Income--His	_____	_____	_____
Employment Income--Hers	_____	_____	_____
Alimony	_____	_____	_____
Pension--His	_____	_____	_____
Pension--Hers	_____	_____	_____
Social Security--His	_____	_____	_____
Social Security--Hers	_____	_____	_____
Dividends	_____	_____	_____
Interest	_____	_____	_____
Capital Gains	_____	_____	_____
Taxable--Other	_____	_____	_____
TOTAL TAXABLE INCOME	_____	_____	_____
NON TAXABLE INCOME			
Child Support	_____	_____	_____
Tax Free Municipal Bonds	_____	_____	_____
Non Taxable--Other	_____	_____	_____
TOTAL INCOME	_____	_____	_____
TAXES			
Federal Income Taxes	_____	_____	_____
State Income Taxes	_____	_____	_____
FICA Taxes	_____	_____	_____
Other	_____	_____	_____
TOTAL TAXES	_____	_____	_____

BEFORE DIVORCE CASH FLOW CONT'D

	CURRENT ANNUAL	CURRENT MONTHLY	% OF GROSS INCOME
NET INCOME AFTER TAXES	_____	_____	_____
COMMITTED EXPENSES			
HOUSING			
Mortgage Payment	_____	_____	_____
Rent	_____	_____	_____
Property Taxes	_____	_____	_____
Homeowners Insurance	_____	_____	_____
Utilities and Fuel	_____	_____	_____
Maintenance/Repair	_____	_____	_____
Other			
TOTAL HOUSING	_____	_____	_____
TRANSPORTATION			
Auto Loan Payments	_____	_____	_____
Auto Insurance	_____	_____	_____
Gas/ Oil/ Repair	_____	_____	_____
Other (commuting, etc)	_____	_____	_____
TOTAL TRANSPORTATION	_____	_____	_____
EDUCATION			
School and College	_____	_____	_____
Other Education	_____	_____	_____
TOTAL EDUCATION	_____	_____	_____
INSURANCE			
Life	_____	_____	_____
Disability	_____	_____	_____
Medical	_____	_____	_____
Other	_____	_____	_____
TOTAL INSURANCE	_____	_____	_____

BEFORE DIVORCE CASH FLOW CONT'D

	CURRENT ANNUAL	CURRENT MONTHLY	% OF GROSS INCOME
OTHER COMMITTED EXPENSES			
Food	_____	_____	_____
Clothing/Cleaning	_____	_____	_____
Phone	_____	_____	_____
Personal Care	_____	_____	_____
Medical Care	_____	_____	_____
Prescription Drugs	_____	_____	_____
Care for Dependents	_____	_____	_____
Repayment of Loans & Charges	_____	_____	_____
Business Meals & Travel	_____	_____	_____
Tax-deductible--Other	_____	_____	_____
Non Tax-deductible--Other	_____	_____	_____
Alimony	_____	_____	_____
TOTAL OTHER COMMITTED	_____	_____	_____
DISCRETIONARY EXPENSES			
Entertainment/Dining	_____	_____	_____
Vacation/Recreation/Club	_____	_____	_____
Other Gifts	_____	_____	_____
Hobbies	_____	_____	_____
Home Improvements	_____	_____	_____
Expenses for Long Term Goals	_____	_____	_____
Miscellaneous Purchase	_____	_____	_____
Tax-deductible--Other	_____	_____	_____
Non Tax-deductible--Other	_____	_____	_____
TOTAL DISCRETIONARY	_____	_____	_____
INVESTMENT OUTLAYS			
IRA	_____	_____	_____
Keogh	_____	_____	_____
Pension Plans	_____	_____	_____
Other Asset Purchases	_____	_____	_____

BEFORE DIVORCE CASH FLOW CONT'D

	CURRENT ANNUAL	CURRENT MONTHLY	% OF GROSS INCOME
TOTAL INVESTMENT OUTLAYS	_____	_____	_____
TOTAL EXPENSES	_____	_____	_____
NET CASH FLOW (negative)	_____	_____	_____

APPENDIX J

AFTER DIVORCE CASH FLOW

	CURRENT ANNUAL	CURRENT MONTHLY	% OF GROSS INCOME
SOURCES OF INCOME			
Employment--His	_____	_____	_____
Employment--Hers	_____	_____	_____
Alimony	_____	_____	_____
Pension--His	_____	_____	_____
Pension--Hers	_____	_____	_____
Social Security--His	_____	_____	_____
Dividends	_____	_____	_____
Interest	_____	_____	_____
Capital Gains	_____	_____	_____
Taxable--Other	_____	_____	_____
TOTAL TAXABLE INCOME	_____	_____	_____
NON-TAXABLE INCOME			
Child Support	_____	_____	_____
Tax Free Municipal Bonds	_____	_____	_____
Non Taxable--Other	_____	_____	_____
TOTAL NON TAXABLE	_____	_____	_____
TOTAL SOURCES OF INCOME	_____	_____	_____
TAXES			
Federal Income Taxes	_____	_____	_____
State Income Taxes	_____	_____	_____
FICA Taxes	_____	_____	_____
Other	_____	_____	_____
TOTAL TAXES	_____	_____	_____

AFTER DIVORCE CASH FLOW CONT'D

	CURRENT ANNUAL	CURRENT MONTHLY	% OF GROSS INCOME
NET INCOME AFTER TAXES	_____	_____	_____
COMMITTED EXPENSES			
HOUSING			
Mortgage Payment	_____	_____	_____
Rent	_____	_____	_____
Property Taxes	_____	_____	_____
Homeowners Insurance	_____	_____	_____
Utilities/Fuel	_____	_____	_____
Maintenance/Repair	_____	_____	_____
Other	_____	_____	_____
TOTAL HOUSING	_____	_____	_____
TRANSPORTATION			
Auto Loan Payments	_____	_____	_____
Insurance	_____	_____	_____
Gas/Oil/Repair	_____	_____	_____
Other (commuting, etc)	_____	_____	_____
TOTAL TRANSPORTATION	_____	_____	_____
EDUCATION			
School and College	_____	_____	_____
Other	_____	_____	_____
TOTAL EDUCATION	_____	_____	_____
INSURANCE			
Life	_____	_____	_____
Disability	_____	_____	_____
Medical	_____	_____	_____
TOTAL INSURANCE	_____	_____	_____

AFTER DIVORCE CASH FLOW CONT'D

	CURRENT ANNUAL	CURRENT MONTHLY	% OF GROSS INCOME
OTHER COMMITTED EXPENSES			
Food	_____	_____	_____
Clothing/Cleaning	_____	_____	_____
Phone	_____	_____	_____
Personal Care	_____	_____	_____
Medical Care	_____	_____	_____
Prescription Drugs	_____	_____	_____
Care for Dependents	_____	_____	_____
Repayment of Loans & Charges	_____	_____	_____
Business Meals/Travel	_____	_____	_____
Tax-Deductible--Other	_____	_____	_____
Non Tax-Deductible--Other	_____	_____	_____
Alimony	_____	_____	_____
TOTAL OTHER COMMITTED	_____	_____	_____
DISCRETIONARY EXPENSES			
Entertainment Dining	_____	_____	_____
Vacation/Recreation/Club	_____	_____	_____
Charitable Contributions	_____	_____	_____
Other Gifts	_____	_____	_____
Hobbies	_____	_____	_____
Home Improvements	_____	_____	_____
Expenses for Long Term Goals	_____	_____	_____
Miscellaneous Purchase	_____	_____	_____
Tax-Deductible--Other	_____	_____	_____
Non Tax-Deductible--Other	_____	_____	_____
TOTAL DISCRETIONARY	_____	_____	_____
INVESTMENT OUTLAYS			
IRA	_____	_____	_____
Pension Plans	_____	_____	_____
TOTAL INVESTMENT OUTLAYS	_____	_____	_____

AFTER DIVORCE CASH FLOW CONT'D

	CURRENT ANNUAL	CURRENT MONTHLY	% OF GROSS INCOME
TOTAL EXPENSES	_____	_____	_____
NET CASH FLOW (negative)	_____	_____	_____

APPENDIX K

LIST OF PRIORITIES

RANK   ITEM

1. _____

2. _____

3. _____

4. _____

5. _____

6. _____

7. _____

8. _____

9. _____

10. _____

11. _____

12. _____

13. _____

14. _____

BIBLIOGRAPHY

Baldwin, Cristina and Brown, Judith. A Second Start: A Widow's Guide to Financial Survival at a Time of Emotional Crisis. New York: Simon & Schuster, 1987.

Caine, Lynn. Lifelines. Garden City New York: Doubleday & Company, 1987.

Caine, Lynn. Widow. New York: Bantam Press, 1985.

Donnelley, Nina Herrmann. I Never Know What to Say: How to Help Your Family and Friends Cope With Tragedy. New York: A Ballantine/Epiphany Book, 1987.

Evicci, Fred W. (editor). The New Social Security. Sacramento, California: Capital Publications, 1987.

Jeffers, Susan, Ph.D. Feel the Fear and Do It Anyway. Orlando Florida: Harcourt Brace Jovanovich, 1987.

Kennedy, David W. Insurance: What Do You Need? How Much is Enough? Tucson: Knight Ridder Press, 1987.

Krantzler, Mel. Creative Divorce: A New Opportunity For Personal Growth. New York, New York: 1973.

Kubler-Ross, Elizabeth MD. Death and Dying. New York, New York: Macmillian, 1970.

Kubler-Ross, Elizabeth MD. Death: The Final Stage of Growth. Englewood, New Jersey: Prentice Hall, 1975.

Kubler-Ross, Elizabeth MD. Living With Death and Dying. New York, New York: Macmillian & Company, 1981.

Lewin, Elizabeth S., CFP. Financial Fitness Through Divorce: A Guide to the Financial Realities of Divorce. New York, New York: Facts on File, 1987.

Martin, Don and Renee. A Survival Kit For Wives. New York, New York: Villard Books, 1986.

Mitchelson, Marvin. <u>Made in Heaven, Settled in Court</u>. Los
Angeles: J.P. Tarcher Inc., 1976.

Porter, Sylvia. <u>Love and Money</u>. New York, New York: William
Morrow & Company, 1985.

Sherman Charles E. <u>How to Do Your Own Divorce in California</u>.
Occidental, California: Nolo Press, 1987.

Wilkie, Jane. <u>The Divorced Women's Handbook</u>. New York, New
York: abcor Press/A Division of Remcoa Inc., 1987.

INDEX